THE FRENCH REVOLUTION

Studies in European History

General Editor: Richard Overy
Editorial Consultants: John Breuilly
                      Roy Porter

PUBLISHED TITLES

T.C.W. Blanning The French Revolution: Aristocrats versus
        Bourgeois?
Peter Burke The Renaissance
William Doyle The Ancien Regime
R.W. Scribner The German Reformation
Geoffrey Scarre Witchcraft and Magic in 16th and 17th Century
        Europe
Robert Service The Russian Revolution

FORTHCOMING

Brendan Bradshaw The Counter Reformation
Michael Dockrill The Cold War 1945–1963
Geoffrey Ellis The Napoleonic Empire
R.J. Geary Labour Politics 1900–1930
Mark Greengrass Calvinism in Early Modern Europe, *c.* 1560–1685
Henry Kamen Golden Age Spain
Richard Mackenney The City State and Urban Liberties, *c.*
        1450–1650
Roger Price The Revolutions of 1848
Clive Trebilcock Problems in European Industrialisation 1800–1930

THE FRENCH REVOLUTION

Aristocrats versus Bourgeois?

T.C.W. BLANNING

**MACMILLAN
EDUCATION**

© T.C.W. Blanning 1987

All rights reserved. No reproduction, copy or transmission
of this publication may be made without written permission.

No paragraph of this publication may be reproduced, copied
or transmitted save with written permission or in accordance
with the provisions of the Copyright Act 1956 (as amended).

Any person who does any unauthorised act in relation to
this publication may be liable to criminal prosecution and
civil claims for damages.

First published 1987

Published by
MACMILLAN EDUCATION LTD
Houndmills, Basingstoke, Hampshire RG21 2XS
and London
Companies and representatives
throughout the world

Printed in Hong Kong

British Library Cataloguing in Publication Data

Blanning, T.C.W.
The French Revolution : aristocrats versus
bourgeois?—(Studies in European history)
1. France—Politics and government—
1774–1793 2. France—Politics and
government—1789–1815
I. Title II. Series
944.04   DC136.5
ISBN   0–333–36304–3

Series Standing Order

If you would like to receive future titles in this series as they are
published, you can make use of our standing order facility. To place a
standing order please contact your bookseller or, in case of difficulty,
write to us at the address below with your name and address and the
name of the series. Please state with which title you wish to begin your
standing order. (If you live outside the United Kingdom we may not
have the rights for your area, in which case we will forward your order
to the publisher concerned.)

Customer Services Department, Macmillan Distribution Ltd
Houndmills, Basingstoke, Hampshire, RG21 2XS, England.

Contents

Note on References

References are cited throughout in brackets according to the numbering in the general bibliography, with page references where necessary indicated by a colon after the bibliography number.

Editor's Preface

The main purpose of this new series of Macmillan studies is to make available to teacher and student alike developments in a field of history that has become increasingly specialised with the sheer volume of new research and literature now produced. These studies are designed to present the 'state of the debate' on important themes and episodes in European history since the sixteenth century, presented in a clear and critical way by someone who is closely concerned himself with the debate in question.

The studies are not intended to be read as extended bibliographical essays, though each will contain a detailed guide to further reading which will lead students and the general reader quickly to key publications. Each book carries its own interpretation and conclusions, while locating the discussion firmly in the centre of the current issues as historians see them. It is intended that the series will introduce students to historical approaches which are in some cases very new and which, in the normal course of things, would take many years to filter down into the textbooks and school histories. I hope it will demonstrate some of the excitement historians, like scientists, feel as they work away in the vanguard of their subject.

The format of the series conforms closely with that of the companion volumes of studies in economic and social history which has already established a major reputation since its inception in 1968. Both series have an important contribution to make in publicising what it is that historians are doing and in making history more open and accessible. It is vital for history to communicate if it is to survive.

R. J. OVERY

Introduction

Few if any inaugural lectures can have had the enduring impact of 'The myth of the French Revolution', delivered by the late Alfred Cobban to University College, London, in 1954 [115 (b)]. It marked the beginning of a controversy about the origins, nature and consequences of the French Revolution which has dominated writing on the subject ever since and which shows no signs of flagging. So voluminous has the literature become, that this short book can do no more than outline the present state of hostilities and suggest how further reading might add substance to the sketch offered.

After thirty years of vigorous argument, consensus is as far away as ever. For the supporters of the 'myth' that Cobban was attacking, the old view still stands like a *rocher de bronze*, despite all the revisionist criticism which has washed around it. In the defiant first words of a recent general history of post-Revolutionary France: 'Despite recent attempts by French, British and American writers to reinterpret the French Revolution, the only plausible, coherent analysis remains that of scholars who, in the tradition of the great French historian Georges Lefebvre, see it as a "bourgeois Revolution"' [139]. Compare that with the equally confident, and even more recent, pronouncement in the volume in the same series which deals with the revolutionary-Napoleonic period: 'Research and reflective criticism over the past twenty years have rendered the classical [Marxist] view of the origins of the Revolution utterly untenable' [129]. As the firmness – not to say trenchancy – of these and a host of other similar verdicts suggests, the controversy has been a dialogue of the deaf.

If scholars who have devoted their lives to the study of

1

French history in the period cannot reach even a modicum of agreement, passing each other unhailed like ships in the night, one might wonder what mere amateurs can hope to make of it all. As we shall see, in fact it is a game we all can play, for 'solutions' depend less on factual knowledge than on presuppositions about such imprecise matters as the course of modern history, social relationships and human nature. One man's 'fundamental insight' turns out to be another man's 'out-dated shibboleth' – and vice versa.

Our point of entry must be the 'myth' which Cobban was attacking in his inaugural lecture. His target can be termed 'the Marxist interpretation', although – as we shall see later – that convenient label covers several different shades of meaning. Its most succinct formulation can be found in a short but penetrating book by Georges Lefebvre: *The coming of the French Revolution* [5]. The essential cause of the Revolution he located in a growing discrepancy between public pretension and economic reality. In legal terms, the old regime was dominated by the first two estates: the clergy and the nobility. It was they who occupied the commanding heights of state and society, it was they who enjoyed all the prestige. In feudal society, when land had been virtually the only form of wealth, their privileged position had had a secure economic base, but by the late eighteenth century it had become an anachronism. For by then the development of commerce and industry had created a new class, the bourgeoisie. Increasingly numerous, prosperous and self-confident, their sense of frustration sharpened by the growing exclusiveness of their social superiors ('the aristocratic reaction'), the bourgeois would not tolerate indefinitely their subordinate position: 'Such a discrepancy never lasts for ever. The Revolution of 1789 restored the harmony between fact and law' [5]. Ironically, it was the nobles who thrust the first battering-ram against the old regime, with their suicidal attack on the absolute monarchy in 1787, thus opening the breach through which the bourgeois poured. As Chateaubriand commented: 'The patricians began the Revolution, the plebeians completed it'.

In other words, the French Revolution represented the

2

decisive stage in the progression from feudalism to capitalism and thus to the modern world. Every country in Europe, of course, made this transition at some stage. What made the French version so special – the greatest revolution in the history of the world, in Marx's view – was its speed, violence and completeness. This radicalism it owed to two interrelated developments. Firstly, there was the determined rearguard action fought by the privileged orders and their foreign allies, in the form of counter-revolution at home and war abroad. Secondly, there was the crucial assistance the essentially timid bourgeois received from the urban masses and the peasants. If the bourgeois had had their way, the Revolution would have been closed down by 1791 at the latest. It was only insistent pressure from below which drove them on to destroy feudalism in its entirety [14].

Yet although separate social strands can be identified, they were not discrete entities but were woven into the seamless whole. Like the acts of a play or the movements of a symphony, the peasant or urban revolutions acquired meaning only when seen as parts of the one and indivisible Revolution. As Albert Soboul, the Lefebvre professor of French revolutionary studies at the Sorbonne, wrote: 'There were not three revolutions in 1789, but just the one alone, bourgeois and liberal, with popular support and especially with peasant support' [13]. Although in a subjective sense the masses may have appeared at times anti-capitalist and at odds with the bourgeois leadership, objectively their participation drove the Revolution on to its goal – the elimination of feudalism.

This was no quick or easy process. The bourgeoisie may have claimed to speak in the name of all humanity, proclaiming universal and eternal truths in the Declaration of the Rights of Man and the Citizen in 1789, for example, but in reality their objectives were narrowly circumscribed. Always prone to compromise with the old order, always seeking to frustrate the genuinely egalitarian and democratic aspirations of the masses, as time passed they allowed their naked class-interests to show through the increasingly revealing garb of revolutionary rhetoric. One crucial stage in this ideological striptease was reached with the coup d'état of thermidor in July 1794, when the revolutionary dictatorship of the

3

Committee of Public Safety was overthrown. Another was the recourse to a military saviour in the shape of General Bonaparte in 1799. Neither of those solutions proved permanent. It was not until 1830 and the July Revolution which toppled the last Bourbon that the French bourgeoisie reached safety, by now not even bothering to pretend that they represented anyone but themselves.

Against this 'classic interpretation', as Soboul called it, the revisionists have launched a series of attacks. At the outset it must be stressed that not all revisionists would subscribe to every individual point of the summary which follows, necessarily painted with broad brush-strokes. Chronologically, the first target has been the nature of social and economic change during the eighteenth century. That the economy expanded is not questioned; that it intensified class-conflict between the nobility and the bourgeoisie most certainly is. The expansion of capitalist enterprise was not the exclusive achievement of the bourgeoisie; on the contrary, many of the most progressive entrepreneurs were nobles [39]. Most bourgeois proved to be positively timid, preferring to invest their capital in land, seigneuries, venal office and government stock [27]. Low in risk – and low in returns – such investments could open the way to the realisation of every bourgeois' dream: the acquisition of noble status. Far from seeking to fight the nobles, the most earnest wish of the *bourgeois gentilhomme* was to join them. It was not difficult to do so. So many ennobling offices were for sale, that anyone with sufficient funds could make the transition [36]. The result was that the French nobility was very numerous; even if the lowest of many possible estimates is taken, the figure (c. 25,000 families) is more than one hundred times larger than that yielded by the British peerage (220 peers in 1790). Far from being an increasingly closed caste, the French nobility was an open elite – too open for its own good, indeed. The 'aristocratic reaction' was a myth [21].

The revisionists have also stressed the heterogeneity of the nobility and the bourgeoisie. So diverse were the members of each group in terms of wealth, position and outlook that neither constituted a class. On the contrary, the upper ech-

4

elons of each came together to form a single elite – 'the notables' – united by wealth and talent [24]. As an alternative label – *l'élite des lumières* – suggests, this fusion found ideological expression in the Enlightenment, not the creed or creation of the bourgeoisie but in large measure the work of the liberal nobility.

If relative harmony ruled among the commanding heights of the old regime, why then did it fall? The answer lies in the fortuitous coincidence of two separate crises at the end of the 1780s. They were not 'discrete' in the sense that each was self-sufficient, for they interacted one with the other, but they were essentially separate [26]. The first crisis was political, deriving from the financial bankruptcy of the monarchy following French participation in the American War of Independence. It brought the virtual collapse of royal government by the summer of 1788 and with it the decision to convene the Estates General. The second crisis was economic, stemming most immediately from the general harvest failure of 1788 but with longer-term origins in population pressure and the recession which had begun in the 1770s [1]. It was the fusion of these two crises in the spring and summer of 1789 which allowed the mass of discontents to become critical and to turn a crisis into a revolution.

What then followed was no class struggle between nobility and bourgeoisie, despite the emotive rhetoric of the Revolution's supporters, but a political contest for power. There were relatively few representatives of the financial, commercial and industrial bourgeoisie at the Estates General: the great majority of the Third Estate's deputies were local officials, professional men and, above all, lawyers [115 (b)]. Moreover, the leaders of the National Assembly – which the Estates General became at the end of June – were nobles, not only in 1789 but throughout the most constructive phase of the Revolution. The sort of France they tried to create was certainly tailored to suit the needs of the bourgeoisie, but would have provided an equally snug fit for the enterprising and wealthy nobles too. In short, it was to be a France created by the notables for the notables.

There are several possible explanations for their failure – in the short term, at least – to achieve this goal. There was

5

the artificial division between noble and commoner created by the manner in which the Estates General were organised [24]. There was the unforeseen and unwanted intervention by the masses, which prompted the bourgeoisie to save their own skins by diverting popular fury against the aristocratic scapegoats [18]. There was the temporary inability of both nobles and bourgeois to look beyond rhetoric to their true interests [120]. There were the persistent economic difficulties which kept the pot of social unrest on the boil. Most crucially perhaps, there was the refusal of the king to play the role allocated to him by the notables, which in turn allowed a group of political radicals to take France into a foreign war [114].

None of these explanations are mutually exclusive. Whatever permutation is preferred, the upshot was that the Revolution was 'blown off course' between 1792 and 1794 [118]. With the compass spinning crazily, this sudden squall brought the abolition of the monarchy, the execution of the king and queen, the attack on Catholicism, counter-revolution, both civil and foreign war, revolutionary dictatorship and the Terror. But the coup d'état of thermidor put the notables back on the bridge, this time for good: political forms may have come and gone, but they stayed on for ever [137].

The France they ruled was a country whose economy had changed astonishingly little as a result of the Revolution. The agriculture of the old regime had been characterised by small units, cultivated by peasants aiming only at subsistence; the agriculture of post-revolutionary France was just the same. The manufacturing sector of the old regime had been characterised by small units, staffed by artisans aiming only at local markets; the manufacturing sector of post-revolutionary France was just the same. Indeed, the changes introduced by the Revolution had been retrograde rather than progressive. The land settlement and the laws of inheritance encouraged fragmentation and kept the peasantry on the land. The monetary chaos of the 1790s, the embargo on British technology and the loss of overseas markets slowed industrialisation. The 'expansion' of the first decade of Napoleon's rule represented only recovery, not a new advance. Most damaging of all, the

6

collapse of overseas trade and the loss of overseas colonies brought poverty to the ports of the Atlantic seaboard and deindustrialisation to their hinterlands [116]. 'Economically', William Doyle has commented, 'the Revolution was a disaster for France' [43].

Certainly France did experience, in due course, a process of modernisation which in certain respects can be termed bourgeois – the creation of a national market, urbanisation, industrialisation, mass literacy, and so on – but it did so in spite of, not because of, the revolutionary legacy. The real destroyer of the old regime was not the Revolution but the railway network constructed more than half-a-century later [43; 141]. Indeed, one influential historian of rural France has dated its transformation to the very end of the nineteenth century [144].

Between these two views of the French Revolution it is difficult to find much common ground. For once, the verbal bitterness of the exchanges between the two groups is in direct ratio to the depth of disagreement [10; 23]. Scholars who have attempted a synthesis only manage to muddle and get muddled. For that reason, no attempt is made in what follows to plane the bumps and smooth the edges of controversy. It seeks only to add some flesh to the bare bones outlined above and thus to allow readers at least to make a start in working out their own conclusions.

1 Origins: the Old Regime

(i) Economic growth and economic problems

'The essential cause of the Revolution', wrote Albert Soboul, 'was the power of a bourgeoisie arrived at its maturity and confronted by a decadent aristocracy holding tenaciously to its privileges' [11]. Born in the first stirrings of a market economy in the middle ages, passing through a troubled adolescence with the overseas discoveries and colonial expansion of the sixteenth and seventeenth centuries, the French bourgeoisie certainly grew in numbers and in wealth in the course of the eighteenth century. The interrelated phenomena of more favourable meteorological conditions, increasing agricultural production and population growth created the necessary conditions for sustained economic expansion.

Beneficent nature was given a helping hand by the state. By providing France with the best network of arterial roads in Europe, so that the time taken to travel from Paris to Lyon, for example, was halved in the course of the eighteenth century, it contributed towards the formation of a national market. By dismantling the restrictive practices of the guilds, it opened the way for capitalist entrepreneurs to exploit growing market opportunities. The rapid expansion of rural industry on a putting-out basis achieved rates of growth comparable to those of Great Britain, even in cottons [40]. Iron production and coal-extraction also recorded spectacular percentage increases. Evidence of the international hegemony of the luxury industries of Paris can still be found in every stately home and museum in Europe.

But the real success story of the French economy in the eighteenth century was overseas commerce. In the Mediterr-

9

anean, French merchants established a near-monopoly of the lucrative trade with the Levant, to such an extent that in 1780 an official memorandum estimated that it sustained between 500,000 and 600,000 people [54]. Even that paled by comparison with the mushrooming colonial sector. From the Atlantic ports, notably Bordeaux, Nantes and Le Havre-Rouen, an ever-increasing merchant marine sailed a triangular route, first to Africa for slaves, and thence to the Caribbean for the colonial produce which fed the apparently insatiable appetites of the rest of Europe. Between the end of the War of the Spanish Succession and the Revolution, French overseas trade at least quadrupled in value, and may have quintupled [40; 58]. Even when the increase in prices, reduction in tariffs and decline in smuggling are taken into account, it can be said that the volume of foreign trade doubled during the same period [131]. Moreover, the expansion of colonial trade was maintained right up until 1789: in 1773 510 ships left eleven French ports for Santo Domingo (by far the most important of the French Caribbean possessions), Martinique, Guadeloupe and Guyana; by 1788 that figure had increased to 686 [60].

But behind these impressive quantitative increases, little if any qualitative change had occurred. Old regime France was a tale of two economies – the prosperous, expanding maritime coasts, together with their shallow hinterlands, and the great mass of the interior, backward, traditionalist and subdivided into largely autarkic local markets [43]. Even the most glamorous sectors, like the colonial re-export trade, did not have sufficient power to draw the rest of the economy into self-sustained growth.

A major obstacle to capital and enterprise flowing from one sector to another was the primitive nature of the financial institutions. For some reason which has never been explained adequately, such modern techniques as bills of exchange, discounting and even double-entry book-keeping came very late to France. More easily explicable, but no less damaging, was the tenacious aversion to banks in the wake of John Law's spectacular bankruptcy in 1720. The old regime knew no state bank, no private bank independent of commerce, no stock exchange and virtually no joint-stock companies [47,I].

Also structurally backward was the manufacturing sector, whose growth statistics look much less impressive when the low base from which they are calculated is taken into account. And when the techniques of production are examined, the qualitative backwardness of French industry is clearly revealed. By 1789, for example, Great Britain had well over 20,000 spinning jennies, 9,000 of the newer mule jennies and 200 mills on the Arkwright model. The equivalent figures for France were: fewer than a thousand, none and eight. Moreover, the great majority of the French machines had been built under the auspices of the royal government and only for the purposes of attracting the special subsidy on offer [57]. In short, the French economy of 1789 was essentially the same as the French economy of 1715 – it was just producing more [40]. Nor was it a story of consistent success even in a purely quantitative sense. Increasing competition from Britain and Central Europe (especially Silesia and Saxony), the protectionist policies adopted by old customers such as Spain and the domestic recession beginning in the 1770s all conspired to send the French textile industry into the Revolution in a debilitated state [35].

Given that some 85 per cent of the French population lived in the countryside, more important was the backward state of agriculture. As the most authoritative estimate suggests that the total population increased from around 22 million in 1700 to around 28 million in 1789 [44] it is evident that there must have been some increase in production. At one time it was argued that this increase was in the order of 60 per cent – about double the rate of population growth – but more recent estimates (and the lack of reliable statistics make them largely a matter of guess-work) place it very much lower [46; 56]. Great or small, most of it was due to an expansion of the acreage cultivated, to previously waste land being put under the plough, not to any rise in *productivity*. Most of French agriculture remained locked in the 'infernal circle of the fallow' (land left fallow = low productivity = high percentage of arable = low percentage of pasture = insufficient livestock = insufficient manure = need for fallow). In 1760 the agronomist Duhamel de Monceau complained that 'almost half the land in this kingdom lies fallow, the other

11

half is generally so badly cultivated that it would bring in at least twice as much if it were properly exploited' [112].

Any landowner or cultivator with sufficient knowledge, capital and enterprise to break out of the circle by the introduction of new crops and new rotations found his way barred by two formidable obstacles. The first was the *servitudes collectives*, the obligation to plant, till, harvest and graze as a community, which ensured that it moved at the pace of its slowest member, i.e. not at all. Sporadic attempts by the government to encourage innovation made little impression [37]. The other obstacle – the inadequacy of communications – was, if anything, more serious and more intractable. Before the railways came, the only cost-efficient way to move grain was by navigable waterways, an asset the French interior notably lacked. It has been estimated that food could not be moved overland further than fifteen kilometres before transport costs devoured the profit margin [141]. The result was wasteful polyculture and an inability to specialise in those crops best suited to a region's soil and climate: for example, in 1789 wine was produced in all but three of the thirty-two *généralités* into which the country was divided [141].

Within this unpromising framework, there was little opportunity and less incentive to engage in the agricultural modernisation needed to allow industrialisation. This picture of rural stagnation should not be overdrawn. In parts of the South-West the introduction of maize allowed yields to be increased; in the North and East – and especially around large towns – new crops were introduced and the fallow eliminated [43]. Not for the first or last time, it is necessary to remind oneself that France was an aggregate of many different economies. Nevertheless, even when the last exception has been noted, the contrast with the agriculture of the Low Countries and Great Britain is very striking.

For the purposes of our present concern, the most important difference lay in the attitude of the landowners. Although improving landlords were to be found, appreciating that a rich tenant meant a rich proprietor, the rate of long-term reinvestment of rural incomes appears to have been low [43]. With market opportunities limited by the inhibiting factors discussed earlier, and with population pressure creating an ever-lengthening queue of would-be tenants and share-crop-pers, the easy way to extra income was through smaller plots and higher rents [48].

So the French economy in the eighteenth century remained predominantly traditional and it is difficult to see how 'the power of a bourgeoisie arrived at its maturity' (see above, p. 9) could be identified within it. It proves even more difficult when the actual aspirations of the bourgeois are considered. It was not the capitalist sectors of the economy which attracted them but the essentially non-capitalist forms of 'proprietary wealth' – land, urban property, venal offices and government stock. It was the first of those – land – which appealed most, partly for its security but mainly for the prestige it conveyed. The bourgeois used their money to buy land which would yield just 1 or 2 per cent, instead of depositing it with merchants who would pay 5 per cent; and they borrowed at 5 per cent to buy land. . .which would yield only 1 or 2 per cent [27]. It has been estimated that at least 80 per cent of the private wealth of France was proprietary in character. Even in the most commercialised of cities it was preponderant: at Bordeaux, for example, there were 700 merchants, brokers and manufacturers, but 1,100 officials, rentiers and property-owners – and many of the merchants held much of their wealth in proprietary form [27].

The other side of the coin was a striking number of enter-prising, innovative noble capitalists. Especially from the 1770s they became 'massively involved' in overseas trading companies and heavy industry [39]. Far from being feudal relics chained to traditional forms of wealth, it was they who were setting the pace in promoting economic change: 'in its most modernising aspects, commercial capitalism was more in the hands of nobles than of bourgeois' [18].

(ii) Social conflict and social fusion

With so many bourgeois behaving like nobles and so many nobles behaving like bourgeois, it is difficult to find much evidence of class-conflict between the two. Indeed it is diffi-cult to identify them as classes at all, whether one adopts a

Marxist definition of class based on economic function and class consciousness or a more general definition such as that proposed by Marc Bloch, who wrote that he would consider those people to be of the same class 'whose ways of life were sufficiently similar and whose material circumstances were sufficiently close not to create any conflict of interest' [34]. No one knows just how many nobles there were, estimates ranging from as low as 100,000 to as high as 400,000. As the apparently endless variety unfolds – among other differences, French nobles could be as poor as church-mice and as rich as Croesus – one can answer in the affirmative Robert Forster's question: 'should we not go a step further and abandon "nobility" altogether as a social category?' [137].

Also ripe for rejection is the notion that the nobility engaged in an 'aristocratic reaction' in the eighteenth century, thus sharpening the bourgeoisie's sense of frustration. Certainly nobles dominated government, administration, the church and the most important social institutions – but they had always done so [21]. If anything, the trend was towards preferring nobles of more recent origin [72]. Where it occurred – and it was not general – the upward revision of seigneurial dues owed more to commercialisation (new bourgeois owners of seigneuries seeking to maximise their investments) than to any feudal initiative [19; 51]. Measures which at first sight betray noble exclusiveness turn out to have been aimed not at non-nobles but at *other* nobles. A classic case was the notorious 'Ségur ordinance' of 1781 which confined admission to the officer corps to nobles with four generations of noble status behind them. This represented a move on behalf of the poor provincial nobility, for whom the army was the chief source of employment, against well-heeled *anoblis* who bought their way up the promotion ladder [36].

This episode highlighted the most corrosive social conflict within the old regime and the most damaging failure of the monarchy. The two most successful and stable states of eighteenth-century Europe – Great Britain and Prussia – owed their success and stability to the integration of their elites, albeit achieved in two very different ways. The task had been facilitated by those elites' relative homogeneity. In France, Louis XIV's creation of an exclusive court, imposition of centralisation and massive expansion of ennobling venal office had saddled the monarchy with a nobility which was too numerous, too diverse and too unintegrated. Languishing in provincial penury and obscurity, the lesser nobility harboured intense resentment of the magnates of the court. Many of them – perhaps as many as a quarter – were too poor even to raise the modest sums required for entry to military service. Their chances of gaining admission to the charmed circles of the magnates were negligible (it was far easier for the daughter of a wealthy *anobli* to marry into a great family than for the daughter of a country squire, however ancient his lineage) [39].

Together with the demoralisation resulting from the monarchy's failures in the course of the eighteenth century, most notably in the all-important fields of war and foreign policy, this growing resentment left the regime friendless when disaster struck at the end of the 1780s. When Louis XVI reached for what should have been his most loyal and most potent weapon – the army – in the summer of 1789, it fell apart in his hands. Without its defection, Jean Meyer has written, the Revolution would have been 'inconceivable' [55].

If anything, the bourgeoisie was even more fissiparous. If it is thought to have been growing rapidly – it may have trebled between 1660 and 1789 [43] – this is due in part to its portmanteau character. For contemporaries, a 'bourgeois' could be a town-dweller, a rentier, a member of the Third Estate, an *anobli*, an economically active and independent commoner, or just a 'boss' [2]. Far from being identified with economically progressive groups, the term was often associated with a person of independent means, as opposed to an active entrepreneur [45]. Of course Marxists are well aware of this diversity: Georges Lefebvre identified five groups (rentiers; officials and lawyers; financiers, shipowners, merchants and manufacturers; artisans and tradesmen; intellectuals, journalists, musicians, artists, etc.); Albert Soboul found four (rentiers; the liberal professions; artisans and shopkeepers; businessmen) [6, 12]. Nevertheless, they are insistent that essentially all these groups constituted a single class:

15

Without doubt the bourgeoisie was diverse and manifold: a social class is rarely homogeneous. But the bourgeoisie was also *one* . . .Top of the list of bourgeois criteria was without any doubt fortune, not so much by virtue of its size as by virtue of its origin, its form, the manner in which it was administered and spent: 'to live like a bourgeois'. There can be no doubt that a Frenchman of the eighteenth century could tell without difficulty whether such and such a person belonged to the aristocracy or stemmed from the bourgeoisie. [13]

But even if Soboul's own criteria are adopted, it is difficult to see how his four categories can be made to form a single class – for the origin, form, management and spending of the fortunes of rentiers, the liberal professions, artisans, shop-keepers and businessmen patently were not '*one*' but very different. The fact of the matter is that the 'bourgeoisie' is a convenient – not to say indispensable – term to designate those commoners who were neither peasants nor labourers, but it did not constitute a class.

Soboul's insistence on the modernity of the leading sector of the bourgeoisie and the confrontational nature of its relationship with the nobility has been criticised by other Marxist historians with a more subtle approach. Régine Robin, for example, has argued that there is more than one way to kill a cat – and more than one route from feudalism to capitalism. More convincing than the class-war model advocated by Soboul and his followers, she suggests, is to see the transition as a process of 'intermingling' *(intrication)*. Before 1789 the relations of production were being transformed in 'the Prussian way', as feudal exploitation made way for capi-talist exploitation with the old elites still in place. Such a pattern is entirely compatible with Marxist theory and, ironically, can accommodate without strain the empirical research of revisionists seeking to deny the validity of that theory. It was Soboul's mistake to try to keep the Revolution as the centre of the transition from feudalism to capitalism and thus to distort its significance [4].

From a rather different – but also Marxist – perspective, Louis Althusser also sought to account for the lack of antagonism between nobility and bourgeoisie during the old regime. He argued that the *industrial* bourgeoisie – 'the true modern bourgeoisie, which transformed the previous economic and social orders from top to bottom' – was unknown to the eighteenth century. Then the most advanced sector was a bourgeoisie which depended on the *mercantile* economy and which consequently was a well-integrated part of the feudal order, with no ambition to fight it. On the contrary, when it acquired wealth, it used it for the purchase of land, venal office, government stock – and noble status. So the order of battle pitched not absolute monarchy against nobles, or nobles against bourgeois, but the feudal regime in its entirety against the masses it exploited. There was a theoretical dispute between king, nobility and bourgeoisie, but a social conflict between the regime and the masses [80]. In fact, as we shall see later, this emphasis on the revolutionary role of the masses accords well with another of Soboul's central arguments.

Whatever one's theoretical point of departure, it is clear that far from fighting the nobles, the bourgeois sought to join them. It was easy to do so – provided the aspirant had enough money. The quickest route was through the purchase of the position of 'King's Secretary', a venal sinecure which conferred immediate and hereditary nobility on the purchaser and his family. Despite the cost – as high as 150,000 livres by the end of the old regime – there were around 2,500 takers (including Voltaire and Beaumarchais) in the course of the eighteenth century [39; 62]. There was a host of other venal offices conferring nobility, although most of them did so only after a period of time. It has been estimated that at least 6,500 families acquired nobility in the course of the century; in other words, about a quarter of the total French nobility was of very recent origin. Significantly, the largest group of these *anoblis* consisted of great merchants, financiers and manufacturers [39]. Neither was there any sign that the urge to social advancement was fading, for between the accession of Louis XVI in 1774 and 1789, 2,477 individuals (including 878 who bought King's Secretaryships) made the leap [36].

These statistics constitute relatively 'hard' evidence of the

17

eagerness of the upper echelons of the bourgeoisie to amalgamate with the nobility. More elusive is evidence of the reverse process. Revisionists such as Chaussinand-Nogaret insist that it was not just a case of the aristocratisation of the bourgeoisie, but also of the embourgeoisement of the nobility:

> From 1760 onward the notions of worthiness and honour, which until then had defined what was special about nobles, were overtaken by a new notion: merit, a middle class value, typical of the third order, which nobility took over, made its own, accepted and officially recognised as a criterion of nobility. From that moment on there was no longer any significant difference between nobility and middle classes. A noble was now nothing but a commoner who had made it. [39]

Such a broad generalisation about such a large number of people is necessarily difficult to substantiate. As we shall see later, the most convincing evidence is retrospective, stemming from the remarkable similarity of the *cahiers de doléances* compiled by the nobility and the Third Estate for the Estates General in 1789. Before that episode can be considered, it is necessary to turn to their joint participation in the progressive cultural movement of the eighteenth century, to the Enlightenment.

(iii) The Enlightenment

In the context of this study, two main questions concern us: can the Enlightenment be termed 'bourgeois'? and what was the relationship between the Enlightenment and the French Revolution? Most Marxist historians give an unequivocal answer to the first: 'In the perspective of social history, the Enlightenment is a historically important stage in the development of western bourgeois thought' [94]. The central ideas of the Enlightenment are identified and are found to correspond to the essential characteristics of the market economy which produced the bourgeoisie. So, for Lucien Goldmann, for example, the principal mental categories needed in a society based on exchange are individualism, contract, equality, universality, toleration, freedom and property and 'anyone who knows the eighteenth century in France will see that this list (and it is no coincidence) is identical with the fundamental categories of the thought of the Enlightenment' [94].

This sort of bird's-eye view, *sub specie aeternitatis*, can accommodate – on its own terms, at least – all the awkward irregularities in the terrain revealed when the focus of vision shifts closer to ground-level. No matter that the philosophes were heterogeneous both ideologically and socially, no matter that large sections of the bourgeoisie were indifferent or hostile to the Enlightenment, *essentially* 'the history of social thought in France in the eighteenth century is above all the history of the development and diffusion of bourgeois ideology and the history of the ideological preparation of the bourgeois revolution' [17]. Not for the first or last time, we reach a point at which mere argument can make no further progress – it becomes a matter of faith. All that can be done is to draw attention to the most important qualifications which suggest that the French Enlightenment did not have a single social identity.

The first place to look, clearly, is at the background of the philosophes. Of course, an examination of a man's social origins provides an inadequate guide to the social nature of his thoughts – the fact that Lenin, for example, came from the nobility hardly justifies labelling Marxism-Leninism as aristocratic. But it does help somewhat. If *all* the philosophes had been bourgeois, the sweeping generalisations such as those by Goldmann and Volguine quoted earlier would be easier to swallow. In the event, one has to choke on discovering that so many of them – Montesquieu, Mably, Jaucourt, Condorcet, Condillac, Vauvenargues, Buffon, Helvétius, Lavoisier, Quesnay, Turgot, Mirabeau (among others) – were nobles. Others turned their backs on their origins by buying their way into the nobility [62]. The list of contributors to the most important single work of the French Enlightenment – *L'Encyclopédie* – includes a high proportion of nobles old and new, a surprising number of clergymen (12 per cent) and in general reveals a cross-section of the upper and middle classes [96]. Moreover, as we shall see later, by the 1780s all the leading lights had been safely assimilated into the high society of the old regime.

If the producers did not form a coherent bloc, neither did the consumers. The *Encyclopédie* did not appeal to the economically progressive sectors of French society, but to the traditional elites – nobles, officials, lawyers and clergymen. Besançon, an old-fashioned provincial capital, with a population of 28,000, provided 338 subscribers to the quarto edition; Lille, an expanding manufacturing centre, with a population of 61,000, provided just 28. As Robert Darnton concludes: 'The readers of the book came from the sectors of society that were to crumble quickest in 1789, from the world of parlements and bailliages, from the Bourbon bureaucracy and the army and the church' [85].

Similar results have been yielded by quantitative studies of two of the main institutional centres of enlightened activity – the provincial academies and the masonic lodges. In the former, 20 per cent of the members were clergymen, 37 per cent nobles and 43 per cent bourgeois. Most of the bourgeois, moreover, were medical men, lawyers, writers and teachers; merchants and businessmen were notably under-represented. The Freemasons were certainly more bourgeois in character, the share of the clergy dropping to 4 per cent and that of the nobility to 15 per cent (22 per cent in Paris). And here, at last, some capitalist bourgeois are to be found, for 36 per cent of the masons in the provinces (17 per cent in Paris) were from banking, commerce or manufacturing [101; 102]. Much work of this kind remains to be done, but it seems unlikely that the revised picture of a socially diverse Enlightenment will be repainted. At the moment we can only conclude with Peter Gay that: 'Our information is too fragmentary and our statistics are too inconclusive to permit any generalisation except one: the consumers of the Enlightenment were distributed across educated society, unevenly but very widely' [92].

More informal but of major importance for the formation and diffusion of enlightened opinion were the salons of the capital. Here more than anywhere was displayed the nobles' adoption of merit as the prime criterion of social value, as both noble and bourgeois intellectuals met to form one like-minded elite. It was a fusion given graphic expression by Lemonnier's justly-celebrated painting of Madame de Geoffrin's salon, in which the intellectual elite of the day – Buffon, D'Alembert, Helvétius, Diderot, Montesquieu, Quesnay, Rousseau, Raynal, etc. – sit side-by-side with great aristocrats such as the Prince de Conti, the Duc de Nivernais, the Duchesse d'Anville and the Maréchal de Richelieu.

This was a relatively early development. From at least the 1730s, admission to the salons was being based more on merit than rank, and progressive nobles – Montesquieu, for example – were engaging freely in social and intellectual intercourse with commoners [103]. It was a process assisted by an education common to the upper echelons of both nobles and bourgeois. In the increasingly meritocratic and competitive world of the eighteenth century, a good education was increasingly prized. As Chaussinand-Nogaret has pointed out:

> To have access to this education was not strictly a privilege of birth, but rather one of wealth. The rich middle classes also took advantage of it, and in the best schools the sons of tax-farmers rubbed shoulders with the sons of dukes and princes of the blood. In this way a cultural elite emerged in which old stock mingled with new blood and magistrates-to-be with officers-to-be. [39]

Even if it is established, however, that the soil from which enlightened ideas grew was a mixture of sand and loam, it does not follow necessarily that those ideas lacked all social character. It is possible, at least, that for reasons of fashion and/or stupidity the nobles espoused ideas inimical to their interests. Two problems confront us here: determining the essential ideas of the Enlightenment, and determining the essential interests of the nobility. The first is the easier of the two. If the French Englightenment was a broad enough church to include within its congregation members as different as Montesquieu and Rousseau, at least some sort of list of unitarian articles can be found. It seems reasonable to conclude, with Peter Gay, that the philosophes wanted a

21

social and political order which would be secular, reasonable, humane, pacific, open and free – free in the sense of 'freedom from arbitrary power, freedom of speech, freedom of trade, freedom to realise one's talents, freedom of aesthetic response, freedom, in a word, of moral man to make his own way in the world' [90].

Conspicuous by its absence from this list is 'equal', for the philosophes were not egalitarian, but meritocratic. Even that should have made them hostile to privileges sanctioned only by birth, but – with a few exceptions – they proved to be remarkably tender towards aristocratic sensibilities. Although unequivocally hostile to such manifest abuses as the game laws, they did not call for the total abolition of the noble order to which so many of them belonged [97]. Real radicalism they reserved for revealed religion.

If it then be asked whether the Enlightenment was hostile to the interests of the nobility, the answer must be conditional on the nature of the noble in question. If he were an intolerant Catholic who set great store by inherited privilege and believed that all was for the best in this the best of all possible feudal worlds, then the new society envisaged by the philosophes was not for him. But if he were confident in his own abilities, and eager to employ them unimpeded by current restrictions, he had every reason to give it a warm welcome. It was a clash of cultures comparable to that depicted by Fielding in the persons of Squire Western and Mr Allworthy.

It is also difficult to see the Enlightenment as unequivocally hostile to the old regime as a whole. The fundamental characteristics of the latter can be summarised as absolutist, Catholic, privileged, hierarchical, particularist (in the sense that loyalties beyond the local community were felt to a province or to the king rather than to an abstraction such as the nation) and agrarian [33]. Of those, only the second can be said to have been rejected axiomatically by the philosophes. Catholicism as an ideology was rejected for its irrationalism, the Catholic Church as an institution was rejected for its wealth, power, corruption and intolerance. Such *causes célèbres* as the Calas and the Chevalier de la Barre affairs periodically gave Voltaire's slogan *'écrasez l'infâme'* fresh urgency [91].

22

Yet in other departments, hostility was directed less towards the essence of the old regime than to its abuses. The only coherent economic theory developed by the French Enlightenment – by the physiocrats – was positively favourable towards agriculture and the land, deemed the only true source of wealth. Their political theories ranged from left to right, from the aristocratic constitutionalism of Montesquieu to the plebeian democracy of Rousseau: 'they all agreed about decency: they were for it. And they all agreed about religion: they were against it. But their political ideas and ideals covered a wide spectrum of possibilities' [92]. If few were as pragmatic as Voltaire, who managed to advocate almost every form of government, depending on which European state he was discussing at the time, no clear programme for political change inimical to the existing political system of France emerged.

In social terms, the story of the philosophes in the eighteenth century is the story of assimilation and integration, not alienation. Their progress is neatly symbolised by two contrasting vignettes: the thrashing Voltaire received in 1726 from the lackeys of the Chevalier de Rohan for poking fun at their master, and Voltaire's triumphant return to Paris in 1778 just before his death, when Parisian high society gathered to celebrate his apotheosis. During the intervening half-century, Voltaire and his colleagues had first infiltrated and then taken over the old regime's cultural institutions, including the *Académie française* in 1772, which they turned into 'a sort of clubhouse' [86]. They had been aided and abetted by a growing number of sympathetic ministers and civil servants, who also ensured that the philosophes' material needs were met by the liberal distribution of pensions. In short, as Robert Darnton has written: 'By 1778, when all of Paris was salaaming before Voltaire, the last generation of philosophes had become pensioned, petted, and completely integrated in high society' [87].

The French Enlightenment was a movement *of* the educated elites *for* the educated elites. With the eternal exception of Rousseau, its most influential representatives did not believe the enlightenment of the masses to be either possible or desirable. Popular education should be confined to the

23

'three Rs' and a measure of physical, occupational and moral training, for its primary purpose was to promote economic utility and social stability, nothing more [84]. In Voltaire's opinion: 'the enlightened times will only enlighten a small number of right-thinking people (*honnêtes gens*). The common people will always be fanatics' – by which he meant attached to religion [98]. Voltaire, of course, was very much a member of the older generation of philosophes – he was born in 1694 – and by the time he made that remark (1759) was very much an establishment figure, but his patrician views were representative of later generations too. Baron Holbach, who lived to see the outbreak of the Revolution and is sometimes described as a democrat, was always careful to distinguish between property-owners and 'the imbecilic masses who, lacking all enlightenment and good sense, can become at any moment the tool and accomplice of subversive demagogues who seek to disrupt society' and demanded 'let us never protest against that inequality which has always been necessary' [100].

If the philosophes are beginning to sound like apologists rather than opponents of the old order, they still had their radical side. In part, this was in spite of themselves. It was one thing to direct their ideas at a restricted sector of society (respectable property-owners), it was quite another to prevent them spreading further. Sir Herbert Butterfield's comment on the effect of the Association Movement in England at about the same time is appropriate here: 'The ideas thrown out by Wyvill and his friends had dropped into a living world and had taken on a life of their own, refusing to dance just to Wyvill's tune or to stop just when he told them to stop.'

It is generally accepted, moreover, that the French version of that 'living world' expanded appreciably in the course of the eighteenth century. The literacy rate for males rose from around 30 per cent in 1680 to around 50 per cent one hundred years later. The criterion adopted to determine literacy is the ability to sign the marriage register, a test which is more reliable than it sounds, for if it over-estimates the number able to write (as well as sign), it *under*-estimates the number able to read at an elementary level [89]. It is probably not without significance that the most literate parts of France

24

were also those which boasted the most ardent support for the Revolution after 1789, namely the North and the East, together with districts anywhere with a high proportion of Protestants (although they, of course, had many other reasons for rejecting the old regime) [105].

It would be absurd, of course, to suppose that peasants or artisans spent their evenings laboriously deciphering Montesquieu's *De l'esprit des lois* or Voltaire's *Dictionnaire philosophique*. It seems clear, however, that at least some of them made the acquaintance of a vulgar – a *very* vulgar – version of the Enlightenment through the pamphlets peddled by street-traders in the towns and hawkers in the countryside. As Robert Darnton has shown, their authors were drawn from an ever-growing literary proletariat, lacking the ability or luck necessary to enter the marble halls of the high enlightenment – and bitterly resenting the fact. Turning their talents to excoriating what they could not join, they produced truly scurrilous *libelles*, so scurrilous indeed that they would certainly be prosecuted for obscenity if published today.

The titillating stories of sexual depravity in high places penned by the *libellistes* in an ever-mounting 'barrage of anti-social smut' (Darnton) were radical in two ways, social and political. In the first place, the guilty parties – the adulterous, promiscuous, incestuous, homosexual, and so on – were invariably members of the 'privileged orders'. Moreover, their essential impotence, and consequent inability to engage in sexual activity except in a perverted form, were often contrasted with the wholesome virility of their servants. The political message was equally clear. As Louis XVI was – of course – depicted as impotent (and not without reason during the early years of his marriage), any number of candidates were suggested in the *libelles* as the sire(s) of 'his' children. Marie Antoinette, on the other hand, was made to play the role of voracious sexual predator, with an appetite for both sexes as indiscriminate as it was insatiable. Typical was the allegation that during the Diamond Necklace affair of 1784 (in which, in fact, she was not involved at all) she had acquired venereal disease from the Cardinal de Rohan and had then infected most of the leading members of the court [86, 88].

25

Of course it is impossible to gauge what readership this socio-political pornography attracted and what effect it had. The strong element of sexual psychopathology which surfaced time and again during the course of the Revolution, however, suggests that it had made a deep impression on the revolutionary crowd's image of the privileged orders and, in particular, of the royal family. When, for example, the Princesse de Lamballe, one of the Queen's alleged lovers, was butchered during the September Massacres of 1792, a crowd set out for the Temple bearing her head on a pike, dragging her body behind and with her bowels carried separately, chanting that Marie Antoinette should be made to kiss the dead lips of her whore. This reputation for depravity pursued her to the very end. At her trial in October 1793, Marie Antoinette was accused not only of treason but also of committing incest with her eight-year-old son and at her public execution the latest *libelles* were on sale, including *Les Adieux de la Reine à ses mignons et mignonnes* [79].

From the well-mannered treatises of the high Enlightenment to the scabrous effusions of the gutter press is a long way indeed, but even in their own elitist world, the philosophes may have been more radical than they intended. This was due less to their own efforts than to the inability of the monarchy to draw the sting of their critique by prudent adaptation. It was more a matter of style than of substance. In actual fact, the regime was more receptive to new ideas and more inclined to reform than it is often given credit for. Not without reason, Alfred Cobban subtitled the chapter on the reign of Louis XVI in his history of France in the eighteenth century 'the age of reform' [66]. Yet, as so often in politics, it was the image projected which mattered most.

For the philosophes, professional writers by definition, the major problem was censorship. Here, as so often, the government contrived to have the worst of both worlds. On the one hand, the ever-growing army of censors (76 in 1741, 178 by 1789) and ever-multiplying censorship regulations (1757, 1764, 1767, 1783, 1785) made life difficult and even dangerous for any author straying beyond the narrow limits of orthodox ideology. Many philosophes (including Diderot and Voltaire) spent time in prison, all of them lived under its shadow [99], On the other hand, the attempt at repression was woefully inefficient. Sabotaged from within – by courtiers such as Madame de Pompadour, no less, and ministers such as Malesherbes, who intervened to protect the philosophes – it only served to stimulate appetites for illicit literature. The travelling-salesman of the *Société typographique de Neuchâtel*, a Swiss-based organisation, reported in December 1780, that it was illegal books which sold best, especially if they had been condemned by the Parlement of Paris. The current best-seller was a work by Raynal, for which there had been a frantic scramble after its well-publicised burning by the public hangman [88]. When Morellet was sent to the Bastille after falling foul of the censors, his friends consoled him by pointing out that imprisonment would make his fortune [99].

So, however much the philosophes may have been assimilated into high *society*, they necessarily remained alienated from *government*. They took its pensions but remained on the outside, looking in – with an increasingly critical eye. Voltaire may have believed that 'the cause of the King is the cause of the philosophes' but the king appeared not to agree. Instructive is a comparison between Louis XVI and Frederick the Great of Prussia. However conservative – even reactionary – the latter may have been, he succeeded in projecting the image of a progressive enlightened moderniser, 'the first servant of the state', in his own well-publicised words. He did so by setting a personal example of tireless public service, as he crossed and re-crossed his scattered possessions, investigating local conditions, chivvying officials and generally maintaining a very visible presence. No less important was his also well-publicised modernisation of the theoretical bases of his state, discarding divine right and dynasticism in favour of the social contract.

It was not the fault of Louis XVI that he was very much less intelligent than Frederick, but not all his failings can be blamed on genetic accident. On only *two* occasions did he stir his ponderous hulk into leaving the Versailles-Paris region: in 1786 when he travelled to Cherbourg to inspect the new harbour installations – and in 1791 when he tried to run away from the Revolution. Symbolic of the musty, old-fashioned flavour of his kingship was the way in which he chose to be crowned. It was his personal decision to insist on the full sacramental panoply, including anointment with the sacred oil of Clovis (originally brought down from heaven by the Holy Ghost, or so it was believed) and an oath to extirpate heresy. Going out of his way to dramatise the extent to which the clock was going back, he revived the ceremony of 'touching for the King's evil' (not performed since 1738), laying hands on 2,400 scrofulous invalids assembled specially in a park and thus claiming semi-divine status as a *roi thauma-turge* [78, 81].

As the philosophes did not subscribe to Christianity, let alone the divine right of kings, it is not surprising that they found it difficult to identify with a regime with ideological foundations such as these [82]. The same could be said of the many members of their constantly growing readership. No matter whether the signs of 'dechristianisation' – decreasing vocations for monastic life and the priesthood, declining popularity of confraternities, diminishing legacies to religious institutions, and so on – denote aversion to the faith *per se* or rather preference for a less baroque form of it, it was an unmistakable phenomenon and at odds with Bourbon concepts of kingship.

As was suggested earlier, the political views of the philosophes were neither cohesive nor revolutionary. Yet, with the possible exception of the physiocrats, they did share a common object of aversion: despotism [104]. By this they meant a debased form of absolutism, the rule of arbitrary, capricious authority unrestricted by law. 'Despotism' was the period's favourite term of abuse and it covered a multitude of sins but, as William Doyle has written: 'Above all, despotism was a charge hurled with ever-increasing frequency at the government and its agents. By the 1780s it almost seemed as if government and despotism were synonyms in the public mind. And this suggests that the old order had lost the confidence of those who lived under it' [1]. It is often stated – rightly – that the monarchy virtually abdicated during the crisis of 1788–9. One can go further and argue that, by failing to adapt both its substance and image to changing conditions, it began this process very much earlier.

With the old focus of authority ruling itself out, progressive political opinion sought an alternative. This it found in abstract concepts known variously as society, the state, the *patrie* or the nation. Although it was only after 1789 that the last of those achieved supremacy and although there was a good deal of argument among the philosophes (especially between Voltaire and Rousseau) over interpretation, in essence they meant the same thing – a secular concept of the public good which all citizens should seek to serve [93]. It was a concept which became increasingly divorced from the monarchy. As the Abbé de Veri observed: 'Today, hardly anyone dare say in Parisian society, I serve the king . . .You'd be taken for one of the chief valets at Versailles. *I serve the state*, is the expression most commonly used' [108].

The political history of France in the eighteenth century is in large measure the history of this bifurcation. It is a subject which demands a book, and a long one, to itself. Here only the major forces separating monarchy from perceptions of national interest can be indicated. During the first half of the century the main issue was religious. By allying with the papacy and associating the monarchy with the attack on Jansenism, Louis XIV and his successors handed to the Parlements, the main institutional source of opposition to absolutism, the priceless opportunity to play the role of defender of Gallican liberties against foreign interference. In the course of this intermittent but often very bitter controversy, the Parlements not only presented themselves as representatives of the national interest but also appealed direct to public opinion through their remonstrances [71]. The effect was to encourage greatly the idea that there existed a centre of loyalty other than the king. As J. S. Bromley has written: 'national sovereignty was the most dynamic concept that was crystallised out of the parliamentary struggle. . .parliamentary Jansenism, and with it what d'Argenson called Jansenist nationalism, did more to shake the fabric of French absolutism, in its theory and its practice, than the philosophers. . .perhaps they [the Parlements] were the real educators of the *sans-culottes*' [65].

Some sharp-eyed contemporaries detected at a remarkably early date what they thought was a decisive shift in the way in which their fellow-countrymen viewed the political process.

Employing a familiar but appropriate image, the Marquis d'Argenson wrote in 1751:

There is a philosophical wind blowing towards us from England in favour of free, anti-monarchical government; it is entering minds and one knows how opinion governs the world. It could be that this government is already accomplished in people's heads, to be implemented at the first chance; and the revolution might occur with less conflict than one thinks. All the orders of society are discontented together. . .a disturbance could turn into revolt, and revolt into a total revolution. [82]

Three years later, when discussing the new-found popularity of such concepts as 'nation' and 'state', he added: 'these two terms were never uttered under Louis XIV; even the idea of them was lacking. We have never been so aware as we are today of the rights of the nation and of liberty'. Observations such as these have led K. M. Baker to suggest that in the course of the 1750s and 1760s 'a radically new political culture' in France emerged, as politics broke out of the absolutist mould [82].

The religious issue faded away in the 1760s, especially after the Parlements' triumph in securing the ejection from France of the Jesuits in 1764. But by now the monarchy had found another potent way to isolate itself from the rest of the nation. In 1756 Louis XV and his ministers reversed the traditional system of foreign policy, which for two-and-a-half centuries had been based on the fundamental axiom of hostility to the Habsburgs, by concluding an alliance with Austria. This was the 'diplomatic revolution'. A *volte-face* of such radicalism might just have been accepted by contemporary French opinion if it had been followed by success; in the event, it was followed by the Seven Years War, during which France lost much of its overseas empire to the British and was humiliated on the continent by the Prussians. The Comte de Ségur was reflecting a general opinion when he wrote:

Thus soon [after 1756] the government no longer possessed any dignity, the finances any order and the conduct of policy any consistency. France lost its influence in Europe; England ruled the seas effortlessly and conquered the Indies unopposed. The powers of the North partitioned Poland. The balance of power established by the Peace of Westphalia was broken. The French monarchy ceased to be a first-rank power. [110]

Memories of this catastrophic collapse of power and prestige were kept alive during the next three decades by further demonstrations of French impotence – the partition of Poland in 1772, Russia's seizure of the Crimea in 1783, Frederick the Great's formation of the League of Princes in 1785, and so on. What little credit that may have been recovered by helping the American colonists to achieve independence from the British was dissipated by the naval and military failures of the last year of the war and the disappointing peace settlement which followed. The *coup de grâce* was delivered by the inability to intervene in the United Provinces in 1787 [114].

On the domestic front, the turning-point for the old regime was reached in the early 1770s with the 'Maupeou revolution' – the attempt by Chancellor Maupeou to reduce the parlements to political impotence [43]. Although stemming primarily from a (successful) manoeuvre designed to discredit Maupeou's political rival, the Duc de Choiseul [69], this *coup d'état* caused a tremendous furore, inspiring a fierce, widespread and sustained debate about the political principles underlying the old regime. The government may have found some support (most notably from Voltaire) but the majority of enlightened opinion, both noble and bourgeois, condemned its actions as despotic. It was particularly ominous that a significant number of critics found neither royalist absolutism nor parlementary aristocracy attractive and looked forward to liberal constitutionalism. In the words of the episode's most recent historian, Durand Echeverria, it 'contributed to a profound and lasting transformation in the way in which the French thought about their government and their society' [70].

In the process of disintegration, more elusive than these specific episodes was the general sense of decay and demoralisation which hung about the monarchy. Partly this was due to that signal lack of charisma of the kings and that isolation and fabled corruption of the court already discussed. It was also due to the chronic indecision and consequent instability which prevailed at the centre. That is revealed by the increasingly rapid turnover of personnel in two of the most important offices of state: the secretary-of-state for war and the controller-general of finance. Between 1715 and 1789 there were eighteen different secretaries-of-state for war; during a similar period in the previous century there had been just five [75].In the all-important department of finance, the situation was even more fluid: between 1715 and 1789 there were no fewer than twenty-five controllers-general of finance, giving an average life expectancy of rather less than three years. Here too, the pace of change was accelerating – seventeen of those twenty-five served between 1754 and 1789, enjoying an average tenure of just over two years. During the last desperate eighteen months of the old regime, six controllers-general were tried, so by then the average was down to just two-and-a-half months! To persuade Louis XVI to take a decision was difficult enough; to persuade him to stick to it was even more of a challenge. The elder of his two brothers, the Comte de Provence, wrote of him contemptuously: 'The weakness and indecision of the King are beyond description. Imagine balls of oiled ivory that you try in vain to hold together' [128].

In this sort of environment, the ideas of the philosophes, however moderate in absolute terms, took on a cutting edge which elsewhere they would have lacked. The point has been well made by Norman Hampson in an illuminating comparison of Burke and Montesquieu and of Dr Johnson and Voltaire. In terms of actual ideas and attitudes, little divided one from the other. What made the Frenchmen so much more hostile to their regime was the fact that they were forced to see themselves 'as a kind of perpetual opposition, with the tendency towards generalised and abstract criticism that the role usually implies' [95]. In short, it was the old regime's inability to adapt which made the French Enlightenment a destabilising force. That was made clear by the response of the élite des lumières to the crisis which began in 1786.

2 Impact: the Revolution

(i) The crisis of 1786–9

By themselves, neither the philosophes of the high Enlightenment nor the muck-rakers of Grub Street could have toppled
the old regime. Once the regime had begun to totter for other
reasons, however, they did get the chance to make their
presence felt. It came at the end of the 1780s. On 20 August
1786 the luckless controller-general of finances of the day,
Calonne, went to tell Louis XVI that the financial situation
was critical. There was an annual deficit of about a hundred
million livres on a total revenue of just 475 million; the third
vingtième, established with considerable difficulty in 1782, was
due to expire in 1787; 1,250 million livres had been borrowed
since 1776 and it had become very difficult to raise more,
even at prohibitive rates of interest. Only radical reform could
stave off total collapse [106].

Thus began a sequence of events which led to the meeting
of the Estates General at Versailles on 5 May 1789. What
occurred during the intervening three years has been
described in many accounts and there is no need to add to
the list here. What does concern us is the social character of
the terminal phase of the old regime and, in particular, the
part played in it by the bourgeoisie.

The traditional interpretation finds the essence of the crisis
in the old contradiction between the reforms the monarchy
needed for its survival and the interests of the privileged
orders on which it depended. The latter were simply irrecon-
cilable with the former, so 'every time a reforming minister
wanted to modernise the State, the aristocracy rose in defence
of its privileges' (Albert Soboul) [12]. But this time the
crown's financial problems were so serious, in the aftermath

33

of the American war, that it had to persevere. That only served to provoke a reaction from the aristocracy even stronger than usual, a full-blooded revolt indeed, which opened the way for the bourgeoisie to move in like infantry behind tanks and to turn a squabble among the feudal elites into a revolution.

There is something to be said for this scheme, but not everything. At least three important qualifications need to be made. In the first place, there was no simple confrontation between would-be modernising monarchy and reactionary privileged orders. As Jean Egret has shown, the Assembly of Notables – summoned in February 1787 to discuss the reforms proposed by Calonne – was not dominated by die-hard defenders of the status quo. There was general agreement that fiscal privileges should be abolished, for example. Where they differed from the king and his advisers was over method. Far from seeking to create a more efficient and more soundly based royal absolutism, the Notables intended to make the most of this golden opportunity to dismantle it. So they made their co-operation conditional on a guarantee that there would be no return to the old mixture of despotism and incompetence [106]. Their dogged resistance, which led to the dismissal of Calonne in April 1787, was not a reactionary move; in the neat formulation of Denis Richet: 'The fall of Calonne was the fall of authoritarian reformism. The hour of liberalism had come' [61].

It was the same liberal determination not to let the absolute monarchy off the hook until permanent *structural* reforms had been conceded that led to the trials and tribulations of Calonne's successor, Brienne, at the hands of the Parlements. Of course it is impossible to be sure when ascribing motives, but it seems clear that when the Parlements called for the convocation of the Estates General or proclaimed that the right to consent to taxation was a fundamental law of the kingdom, they were not just defending narrow class-interests but were also advancing principles which they believed to be essential to the national interest.

Needless to say, not all French nobles and clergy marched around in one great Gladstonian army of earnest liberals. There were enough reactionaries among them of the 'never-

34

give-an-inch' variety to give some semblance of reality to the sort of aristocrat who appears in Jacobin rhetoric, Charles Dickens' *A Tale of Two Cities* and Albert Soboul's *History of the French Revolution*. Even so, the number of nobles in the vanguard of radical agitation during this period is very striking. During the winter of 1788–9 a group known as the 'Society of Thirty' met regularly to co-ordinate the opposition's campaign in the elections to the Estates General. Its leaders were almost all nobles – among them, the Duc d'Aiguillon, the Duc de la Rochefoucauld, the Duc de Lauzun, the Marquis de Lafayette, the Marquis de Condorcet, the three Comtes de Lameth, the Comte de Mirabeau and the Vicomte de Noailles. Of the fifty-five members whose identity has been established, only five were commoners [113].

A further – and very important – qualification has to be made about the nature of noble aspirations in 1789, as revealed by the *cahiers de doléances*, the remonstrances drawn up nation-wide in each *bailliage* for consideration by the Estates-General. A crucial issue was whether voting at the latter should be by order (which would have given a built-in majority to the clergy and nobility) or by head (which would have done the same for the Third Estate). Far from forming a united bloc against the Third Estate, the nobility divided. Only 41.04 per cent of the *cahiers* supported mandatory voting by order, results achieved often only after fierce debate and by small majorities. That figure was almost matched by the 38.76 per cent of the cahiers which actively supported or at least were prepared to accept voting by head. The remaining *cahiers* opted for voting by order, but did not make it an inflexible principle, or were selective (demanding voting by order for certain issues, by head for others) [39].

Even more striking was the coincidence of the views of the nobility and the Third Estate on how France should be reformed. Taking a representative sample of liberal demands, Table 1 shows that, if anything, the nobles were *more* liberal than their bourgeois colleagues. Certainly it is impossible to infer any confrontation between two diametrically opposed classes. This sort of table provides the revisionists with their best evidence of the pre-revolutionary fusion between noble and non-noble elites. It makes clear that both groups wanted

Table I
Liberal Nobles in 1789

Cahiers de doléances which supported:	of the nobility %	of the 3rd estate %
Equality before the law	23	17
Abolition of *lettres de cachet*	68.65	74
Abolition of interference in the judicial procedure by the government	47	40
Introduction of Habeas Corpus	40	31
Giving accused legal representation	24	35
Insistence on the establishment of a constitution as a precondition of any further grant of taxation	64	57
Division of legislative power between the king and the Estates General	52	36
Giving legislative power to the Estates General only	14	20
Regular meetings of the Estates General	90	84
Parliamentary immunity	24	16
Control of taxation to the Estates General	81	82
Fiscal equality	88	86
Ministerial responsibility to the Estates General	73	74
A constitutional regime in general	62	49
Liberty of the Press	88	74
Freedom of commerce	35	42
Abolition of monopolies	59	72
More economic freedom in general	45	66
Abolition of seigneurial rights	14	64

[18, 39]

the same solution to the country's problems: a moderate, peaceful change to a modernised constitutional monarchy, for their mutual benefit [18].

What is more, these liberal words of the nobles were supported by action. As was pointed out earlier, it was nobles who played the leading part in the Society of Thirty during the winter of 1788–9. It was also nobles who played the leading part once the Estates General had met. About ninety noble deputies, a third of the total, can be classified as liberal, and to them should be added several more sitting in the other two Estates. They quickly made their mark: it was the Comte de Mirabeau who emerged as the leader of the National Assembly (which the Estates General became at the end of June 1789), it was the Marquis de Lafayette who became the first commander of the Paris National Guard, it was the Vicomte de Noailles who introduced the decrees abolishing 'feudalism' on 4 August 1789, it was Talleyrand (a bishop as well as a noble) who proposed the secularisation of church land, it was the Comtes de Lameth who helped to found the Jacobin Club, and so on and so forth.

All this is well known. What is more often overlooked is the crucial role played by nobles in the collapse of the monarch's last line of defence – the army. Demoralised by the catastrophes of the Seven Years War, disaffected with a foreign policy at odds with what they conceived to be the national interest, exasperated by the constant chopping and changing of military regulations, bitterly resenting the venal system which allowed wealthy young men to buy their way up the promotion ladder, the officer corps was in a thoroughly alienated frame of mind by the late 1780s [63].

They were made positively mutinous by yet another attempt to revamp the system beginning in 1787, under the direction of the Comte de Guibert, the most unpopular man in the French army. To the fore in the demonstrative sabotage of this exercise were men like the Lameth brothers, Lafayette and Lauzun, soon to make their mark as revolutionary politicians. Indeed, it is striking just how many liberal nobles were also army officers: in addition to the names just listed, there were Clermont-Tonnerre, La Rochefoucauld-Liancourt, La Rochefoucauld-Enville, Noailles, Aiguillon,

Dillon, Mirabeau, and many more [73; 75]. So when the king tried to use his army to suppress disorder in 1788–9, too many officers were too unreliable for his attempt at coercion to succeed. As Lafayette observed, it was the officers 'who gave their soldiers the first lessons in insubordination' [73]. When it is also recalled that more than half of the noble deputies at Versailles – 154 – were army officers, it could be argued that the French Revolution was in part a military putsch. As Comte Miot de Melito observed: 'the defection of the army was not one of the causes of the Revolution, it was the Revolution itself'.

If the nobility and the upper echelons of the bourgeoisie were so united in their wish to see a moderate and peaceful transformation of the old regime, it must now be asked why the leaders of the Third Estate employed such hostile language against the nobility and how it was possible for Mallet du Pan, for example, to make the often-quoted remark early in 1789: 'The public debate has changed. Now the King, despotism, the constitution are merely secondary: it is a war between the Third Estate and the other two orders.' The answer lies in the conflict created by the decision of the Parlement of Paris that the Estates General should meet in the form current when it last convened – in 1614. This led to many nobles of recent origin – the *anoblis* – being depressed into the Third Estate, and bitterly resenting the fact [24]. It also led the liberal nobles of the Society of Thirty to agitate for abolition of the 'forms of 1614', a campaign which proved counter-productive, for it only served to provoke the more conservative members of the privileged orders to take up entrenched positions under the banner of 'no concessions' [1]. It was an artificial conflict which was thus created, not a true conflict of interest, but it was to be many years before the rift could be healed and the noble-bourgeois elite reassembled in the shape of the post-revolutionary notables.

The delay was occasioned by the same force which made the Revolution so radical and so violent. It was the sudden eruption on to the national scene of the masses. Although their grievances were social and economic in character, their campaign to secure redress was to have profound political consequences. Its manifold long- and short-term origins have been examined in great detail by scores of scholars, and here only the briefest of outlines can be given.

If the single most important cause of the socio-economic crisis of the old regime has to be identified, then population pressure has the best credentials. The growth rate in the eighteenth century of rather less than 30 per cent was actually rather modest by contemporary standards (Great Britain's figure, for example, was more than double that) but France was, relatively speaking, a densely populated country even before the eighteenth-century increase began [47]. While there was still waste land to be put under the plough, while the harvests remained good, while the commercial and manu-facturing sector remained buoyant – as was generally the case during the middle decades of the century, despite occasional hiccoughs – the surplus could be absorbed without too much difficulty. Even so, the trend was towards pauperisation, as both the number and proportion of peasants with midget plots or no land at all constantly grew. For everyone unable to grow all the food he and his family required – for the great majority, in other words – the standard of living was deteriorating, for the law of supply and demand sent up the price of food at the same time as it depressed the reward for labour: between the 1730s and 1789 prices increased three times faster than wages [107].

This secular trend was intensified from the late 1770s by a recession which affected all sectors of the economy except colonial trade. It had been a difficult decade altogether, with a subsistence crisis sparking off the 'flour war' in 1775, the most serious peasant rising before the Revolution. But it was the collapse of wine prices three years later, due to over-production and over-abundant harvests, which heralded a period of prolonged misery for the peasantry. Wine was so important a cash crop for so many peasants that this disaster had serious repercussions for the rest of the economy.

In the mid-1780s this enduring problem was intensified by bad weather which variously decimated forage crops together with the animals which depended on them, and ravaged industrial crops together with the manufacturers who depended on them. In this pre-industrial economy the interaction between the dominant agricultural sector and manufacturing was automatic and swift. A sudden increase in the price of food brought an equally sudden collapse in the demand for manufactured goods; that led necessarily to an equally sharp contraction in the demand for labour – just at a time when both peasants and urban labourers needed employment more than ever to cope with the higher prices. It was only those lucky peasants able to grow more than they needed for survival who flourished in such conditions – but they were in a small minority. As if this were not enough, there were some special problems afflicting the economy in the late 1780s, among them the Eden Treaty of 1786 which exposed French markets to British competition, a damaging trade dispute with Spain, and the war in the Baltic between Russia and Sweden which shut off the granaries of Prussia and Poland just when they were needed most.

Contemporaries were convinced that poverty and its associated problems were getting worse in the 1780s and all the evidence suggests that they were right. The most visible and alarming sign was the galloping expansion of groups on the margin of society, of foundlings, prostitutes, beggars, vagrants and criminals. Gangs of bandits more numerous, larger and more violent than anything seen in the past, terrorised the countryside with highway-robbery, burglary and extortion [50].

So it was an old regime both debilitated by deprivation and accustomed to social violence that the final disaster struck in the summer of 1788. In twenty-seven of thirty-two *généralités* the harvest failed, thus creating a subsistence crisis of unprecedented scope and severity. The result was that prices began to rise just when they should have been coming down and went on rising throughout the autumn and winter of 1788–9. It has been estimated that a working man in Paris could keep his family above the bread-line only if the price of bread kept below two sous a pound; by July 1789 it had reached four sous a pound [5]. Perhaps even more inflammatory was the commonly-held belief in a *pacte de famine*, a monstrous conspiracy by government and grain-dealers to make their fortunes at the expense of the people.

The news that the Estates General were to meet, the agitation surrounding the election of deputies and the discussion

40

of grievances to be included in the *cahiers* all helped to raise the temperature even higher. All over France, both urban and rural violence increased, reaching a climax in July 1789 with the 'Great Fear' in the countryside and the storming of the Bastille at Paris. It was at this point that the catastrophic consequences of the unreliability of the army made their full impact. If Louis XVI had been able to disperse the Estates General (or the 'National Assembly', as it styled itself after 17 June 1789) and to restore order in Paris, he might well have been able to prevent what turned out to be the fatal fusion of the political crisis with the socio-economic crisis. Of course a coercive exercise could not have solved the financial problems of the monarchy but it would have won a vital breathing-space, for once the new harvest had been brought in, the social temperature would have dropped.

That is speculation. In the event, the 17,000-odd troops which could be moved from the frontier (characteristically, they were in the wrong place at the wrong time) only made matters worse. On the one hand, news of their assembly sent the temperature past boiling-point; on the other, they could not be used for fear that they would mutiny [109]. When the revolutionary crowd attacked the Bastille, they were not seeking to liberate political prisoners or to destroy a symbol of the old regime, they were looking for arms and ammunition with which to equip their new para-military force – the National Guard. That is the true importance of 14 July 1789 – it marked the collapse of the regime's most valuable asset: its monopoly of disciplined armed force. Once that monopoly had been broken, the Revolution had come to stay.

(ii) The Revolution and the new order

'By their fruits ye shall know them' (Matthew, vii. 20): on the face of it, an obvious test for the identification of the social character of the French Revolution would be an analysis of what the revolutionaries did when they came to power. That, surely, would shed light on the nature of their grievances and aspirations under the old regime. Unfortunately, it seems clear – to revisionist historians, at least – that the ideology

41

of the revolutionaries was actually forged during the revolutionary crisis itself and that a sharp break occurred in 1789. The evidence of the *cahiers de doléances* suggests that the Enlightenment had not created a revolutionary mentality, that most people wanted moderate reform and that very few had any idea just how radical the Revolution would turn out to be. As George Taylor has argued: 'the revolutionary state of mind expressed in the Declaration of the Rights of Man and the decrees of 1789–91 was a product – and not a cause – of a crisis that began in 1787' [111]. In short, it was not the revolutionaries who made the Revolution but the Revolution which made the revolutionaries [1].

Nevertheless, even if it was the case, in the words of François Furet, that 'the revolutionary event, *from the very outset*, totally transformed the existing situation and created a new mode of historical action that was not intrinsically a part of that situation' [23], it is both legitimate and necessary to look at what the Revolution actually did. As soon as one does, one cannot help but be struck by the extent to which it furthered the interests of the bourgeois. At both a national and a local level it was they who benefited most from the new political arrangements. The electorate was divided into three – 'passive citizens', 'active citizens' and 'eligible electors' – on a sliding scale of wealth which in effect gave political power to the prosperous. Theoretically, a simple material criterion should have favoured nobles just as much, but in practice they dropped out of sight in the political life of most of the eighty-three departments into which France was now divided [129]. The great number of regional studies, which in most respects have stressed the heterogeneity of revolutionary France, have confirmed in detail that in one community after another it was the bourgeois who took control [for example, 117, 124, 127]. This was not a fixed group, of course. On the contrary, the new men were in turn replaced by newer men, with the result that a large number acquired some kind of direct political experience in the course of the 1790s [121].

This new political class can be defined as 'bourgeois' in a loosely Marxist sense, both in terms of social position and class consciousnesss. Although various in terms of economic function, its members did own the means of production, whether in the form of capital, skills, tools or land. Although various in terms of political opinion, its members did unite in their rejection of feudalism, aristocracy and absolutism. Unfortunately, to use 'bourgeois' in this way does not take us very far. Such a capacious category cannot distinguish between militant republicans and moderate royalists. Neither can it accommodate the awkward fact that the most advanced parts of France, economically speaking, were often right-wing, while radical republicanism was most intense in the least capitalist regions [121].

Nevertheless, the social and economic policies of the National Assembly were also manifestly favourable to the bourgeoisie. In the meritocratic society they created, it was men of means and education who enjoyed a head-start. The revolutionaries may have used universalist rhetoric – may even have believed that they were acting in the interests of all – but it was clear who stood to benefit most. Even the Declaration of the Rights of Man and the Citizen, the most self–consciously universalist of all the revolutionary documents, declared private property to be a natural and inalienable right (a principle of little relevance to the great majority of Frenchmen who owned no property and had no prospect of doing so) [12]. The abolition of internal customs barriers, the abolition of privileged trading monopolies, the introduction of a uniform system of weights and measures, the method adopted for the sale of the *biens nationaux*, the Allarde law which abolished guilds, and the Le Chapelier law which outlawed workers' associations, all promoted bourgeois interests. On a more symbolic level, the abolition of noble titles and such honorific noble privileges as the right to bear arms and to sport heraldic devices, the introduction of 'citizen' as the approved form of address, and many more changes of the same stamp combined to elevate the bourgeoisie's social status.

But did these changes promote *only* bourgeois interests? Were not the enterprising nobles equally – or even additionally – favoured by the dismantling of the old regime's restrictions? The nobles were also men of means and education, indeed men of more means and better education than most of their bourgeois competitors. In exchange for abandoning a number of honorific privileges, to which many of them attached no importance anyway, they were now offered limitless opportunities for political and material advancement. Of course many nobles regarded the Revolution as the devil's work and could not even bring themselves to live in France while it lasted, but for every Comte d'Artois who demonstratively emigrated, there were a dozen who stayed at home and quietly got on with making the best of it. Only between 7 and 8 per cent of French nobles emigrated and not even all of them can be classified as unequivocally reactionary [120].

Attention is usually drawn to the number of nobles who emigrated, but more striking is the number of nobles who gave their active support to the Revolution, even during its most terrorist phase. The experience of the officer corps, the body most self-consciously devoted to old-regime values, is instructive. It is certainly the case that about 60 per cent of the officers had emigrated by the time war broke out – but what is more impressive is the fact that 3,000 remained. The revolutionary armies which gained the first great victories and conquests in 1792 were commanded by former nobles: Dumouriez, Montesquiou and Custine [109]. Despite repeated purges, there were still 900 noble officers serving in September 1793, a figure which was depleted during the Terror of year II (1793–4) but which rose again in 1795 to over a thousand, a hundred of whom were generals [120].

In the civilian sphere too, the degree of continuity is striking. Of the fifty-eight presidents elected by the Constituent Assembly, thirty-one were nobles [18]. And if noble representation was appreciably smaller in subsequent legislatures, it was still there. Even after the abolition of the monarchy, there were still forty nobles in the National Convention, many of them very radical and many of them leading lights (Condorcet, Kersaint, Barras, Hérault de Séchelles, Soubrany, Le Peletier de Saint Fargeau) [120]. One can even call on the experience of *counter*-revolutionaries to show how tenacious was noble support for the Revolution. The Comte de Puisaye, for example, the leading counter-revolutionary commander in the West of France in 1794–5, gave the Revolution his active support until as late as the summer of 1793, distributing trees from his estate to serve as totems of liberty, standing as godfather to the children of local patriots, playing a leading role in the local National Guard and standing for election to the National Convention [122].

By the time the Comte de Puisaye abandoned the Revolution, France had been plunged into the Terror of year II (1793–4). It was an episode which continues to generate intense controversy and a huge literature. It has been seen by Marxists such as Albert Soboul as the natural and inevitable climax of the Revolution, a time when the masses – led by the *sans-culottes* – drove the timid bourgeois on to complete the destruction of the feudal order [12]. Yet it was essentially an aberration, an exceptional reaction to an exceptional emergency. The military defeats of the spring of 1793, the consequent threat of foreign invasion, the sharply deteriorating economic situation and the counter-revolutionary insurrections all conspired to unleash a campaign of state-terror to mobilise every last national resource, both human and material, in defence of the Revolution. Once that objective had been achieved, by the summer of 1794, the way was clear for a return to normality. As François Furet has observed: 'Far from being an inevitable part of the revolutionary process, the dictatorship of Year II bears all the marks of contingency, of a nation that had found itself in dire straits' [118]. Moreover, the chief victims of the Terror were the bourgeois merchants and manufacturers.

Further doubts about the bourgeois nature of the Revolution are aroused when the beneficiaries are examined. They are difficult to find. Taking 1799 as one's vantage-point, the only groups that can be said to have benefited in a material sense from the Revolution were purchasers of *biens nationaux* and the army (or, rather, those members of it who had both won promotion and had survived). Certainly the bourgeois were to the fore in the former group. The original regulations were designed to favour small proprietors – purchasers had to find only 12 per cent of the price immediately and could pay off the rest in twelve annual instalments at 5 per cent interest. Subsequent changes increased the deposit, reduced the repayment period and increased the interest rate, with the result that only the richer peasants and, above all, the bourgeois were in a position to take advantage of the system [48]. As Denis Woronoff has pointed out, when the dust settled at the end of the 1790s: 'it was the merchants, industrialists, solicitors and lawyers who emerged victorious from this contest, with the not-disinterested help of the administrators of the *départements*' [130]. Yet, paradoxically, this bonanza only confirmed the French bourgeoisie's conservative predilection for proprietary wealth. The combination of the abolition of venal office and the availability of vast tracts of land only served to make land – rather than manufacturing, finance or commerce – even more popular for bourgeois investors.

Indeed, the economic conditions created by the Revolution were singularly unconducive to capitalist investment. Prominent on the long list of those who lost as a result of the Revolution were bourgeois capitalists, for whom the 1790s were years of great difficulty. A particular and enduring problem was the new regime's monetary policy. Galloping inflation, caused by the reckless printing of money, reached a climax in 1796 when it was costing more to print the *assignats* than they were worth. But the abandoning of paper money was followed by sharp *de*flation, a collapse of agricultural prices, a shortage of cash and high interest rates, causing problems for the business community which were different but just as intense [59].

The need to resort to paper money had been magnified greatly by the war, and it was the war which was mainly responsible for plunging the manufacturing sector into recession, by disrupting the supply of raw materials and by blocking access to foreign markets. From one textile manufacturing centre after another came the cry that output had fallen precipitously: Lyon had had 12,000 looms in 1789, but only 6,500 in 1802; Carcassonne's production had fallen from 60,000 rolls of cloth to just 17,000 or 18,000; by 1801 Le Mans had only 100 *métiers battants* left, compared with 274 in 1788, and production had declined in proportion; in the linen-producing regions of Brittany, production had fallen by at least a third in the course of the decade; the value of industrial production at Marseille fell by three-quarters after 1789, and so on [123; 131; 136]. The most recent historian

46

of French textiles sums up as follows:

> The Revolution brought disaster to the French textile trade
> in every imaginable form: currency disorders, radical
> changes of fashion in clothing, loss of foreign customers,
> severe raw material shortages. Hundreds of thousands of
> cottagers were forced to abandon the trade; bankruptcy
> swallowed up hundreds of merchant houses. [57]

That catalogue of disasters could be matched, and even added
to, by merchants engaged in overseas trade. Once Great
Britain had entered the war, in February 1793, French ports
were blockaded by the Royal Navy. The statistics illustrating
the consequences are even more devastating than those relat-
ing to manufacturing: by 1797 there were only 200 ocean-
going vessels left, a tenth of the 1789 total; by 1799 French
exports amounted to 272 million francs, just half of the
1789 figure, even though in the meantime Belgium and its
relatively advanced economy had been annexed; in 1789
foreign trade accounted for 25 per cent of the country's gross
physical product, by 1796 it had fallen to 9 per cent; and so
on [123, 125].

This sharp decline of manufacturing and commerce led to
two phenomena known inelegantly as deindustrialisation and
deurbanisation. Particularly in the industrial hinterland of
those ports which had boomed during the eighteenth century
there was a pronounced shift in the economic balance away
from manufacturing [116]. The difficulty in finding alternative means of livelihood, especially at a time when the Revolution had eliminated so many forms of proprietary wealth,
was reflected in the declining populations of major cities.
Between 1789 and 1806 the population of Paris fell from
more than 650,000 to 581,000, of Marseille from 110,000
to 99,000 and of Bordeaux from 110,000 to 93,000 [44].

It seems an odd sort of bourgeois revolution that can inflict
such damage on the most advanced sector, economically
speaking, of the bourgeoisie. This is an argument, however,
which must be treated with caution. The revolutionaries who
destroyed the old regime and erected the new did not know
that in April 1792 they would become involved in a war

which would last for the best part of a quarter of a century. On the contrary, the early pronouncements by the revolutionaries on the subject of foreign policy were entirely pacific. It was not until the autumn of 1791 that the possibility of war arose, thanks to the ambition of the Brissotins, the treachery of the Court and the miscalculations of the Austrians and the Prussians [114]. Once they found themselves 'trying to run a twentieth-century war effort with means available to a pre-industrial society' [119], as Norman Hampson has put it, the over-exertion involved inevitably wreaked havoc with the economy. In short, one should not infer motives from consequences.

It might also be objected that a perspective longer than a decade is required to assess the social and economic effects of the Revolution. However deep the wounds inflicted by the war, sooner or later they were bound to heal, allowing the long-term benefits to assert themselves. It is to this aspect that the following and final section is devoted.

3 Aftermath: Napoleon and Beyond

The development of France in the post-revolutionary period is characterised by what Georges Lefebvre described as a 'gigantic paradox'. Although the country had experienced 'the greatest revolution in the history of the world' (Karl Marx), in economic terms nothing seemed to have changed much. The political and social institutions of the old regime – the absolute monarchy, noble privileges, the established church – had been torn up by the roots, but the economy trundled along on its ponderous path more or less unaffected. It was all very well to blame the delay on the inevitable birth-pains of a new order or on the effects of the war, but such excuses were wearing thin a hundred years later, for – as Clive Trebilcock has written – 'by 1900 France was clearly the economic laggard among the powers and not even the unusually energetic progress of the *belle époque* could erase the languid and spasmodic growth pattern of the preceding century and a half' [142].

If the French bourgeoisie really had entered into their kingdom in 1789, then they took their time about exploiting their economic advantages, as the rates of growth achieved in France during the nineteenth century were substantially below those of other industrialising countries. Every attempt to argue that the French economy was not so backward after all [134; 138] founders on the rock of relativity. In the course of the nineteenth century France fell behind the USA, Germany, Austria-Hungary and Russia in terms of population; in terms of total industrial production, France was overtaken by the USA, Germany and Great Britain and in terms of real income per capita by Switzerland, the Nether-

49

lands, Belgium, Scandinavia and several parts of the British Empire as well [133]. Contemplation of the superior growth rates achieved by the economies of Great Britain and Germany, where so many features of the old regime survived, suggests that when it came to industrialisation, a revolution of the French variety was at best an irrelevance and at worst a handicap.

The temptation to view the Revolution as anti-capitalist in its consequences must be tempered by the consideration that the pace of industrialisation in France might have been even more lethargic without it. Great Britain and Germany, after all, enjoyed superior natural communications and superior natural resources. Nevertheless, it does seem clear that, from being roughly on a par economically on the eve of the Revolution, France and Great Britain had diverged appreciably by 1815. The economic recovery of the Napoleonic Empire had been just that – recovery to the old regime's levels of output after a decade of deprivation [141]. Many of the industries which flourished – notably textiles – could do so only in the artificial conditions created by protective tariffs and the economic domination of the rest of the continent that went with French military hegemony. When the rest of Europe regained its independence and when British goods regained access to French markets, the hothouse flowers (already nipped back by the sharp recessions of 1810–11 and 1813–14) withered accordingly. As François Crouzet has concluded: 'France was not disastrously behind [in the 1780s], and the Industrial Revolution might have taken off there with only a few years' delay in relation to England. But the "national catastrophe" which the French Revolution and the twenty years war meant to the French economy would intensify the discrepancy and make it irremediable' [40].

The negative effects of the 'national catastrophe' were enduring. The 1,300,000 Frenchmen lost as a result of the wars between 1792 and 1815 left the country with a low male/female ratio (down from 0.992 in 1790 to 0.857 in 1815) and a falling share of Europe's population [44]. The agrarian policies of the Revolution only served to confirm and consolidate the predominance of peasant-proprietors aiming just at subsistence agriculture. The bitter legacy of politi-

50

cal and social polarisation, which brought repeated violent changes of regime and a persistent sense of instability, almost certainly helps to explain the fabled and fatal reluctance of Frenchmen to invest in domestic enterprise. The contrast in this regard with Great Britain (or even Germany) in the same period is both striking and instructive.

It is just this constant reference to the contrasting experience of the British economy which has attracted the criticism of a group of Marxist-Leninist historians. The most influential of them has been Anatoly Ado, whose *magnum opus* – a study of peasant movements in France between 1789 and 1794 published in 1971 [30] – has not been translated from its original Russian but has been immensely influential. It was Ado's invaluable service to his Marxist-Leninist colleagues to demonstrate how the 'gigantic paradox' which had troubled Georges Lefebvre could be overcome. Indeed, he was sharply critical of certain important aspects of Lefebvre's work on the peasants. In particular, he argued that Lefebvre had been quite wrong to conclude that the peasant revolution was not an integral part of the bourgeois revolution. In Ado's view, that fundamental error had led Lefebvre to the equally mistaken conclusion that the peasants' programme was in many respects hostile to economic progress and that therefore the peasant revolution had been – and this was the 'gigantic paradox', of course – both revolutionary and conservative [30].

Ado resolved the problem by distinguishing between the subjective and the objective roles of the peasantry. In a subjective sense, the peasants' deeds and words may have appeared to have been anti-capitalist, backward-looking, designed to protect their traditional communal rights and structures. But *objectively*, by demanding, fighting for and eventually achieving the total destruction of feudalism, the peasants opened the way for the triumph of capitalism. It was the democratic, egalitarian way, but it was the way to capitalism just the same. Their creation of free peasant property led to a differentiation between property-owners and labourers and the possibility of capital accumulation. Ado was also at pains to stress the crucial importance of the peasant movement. It was no separate epiphenomenon but the true motor of the Revolution, right from the very start: 'the popular movements played the most decisive, dynamic role in bringing about the development of the revolutionary crisis [in 1788–9] and its transformation into a revolution' [30].

So, far from being a conservative force, the peasant movements in France were as radical as it was possible to be. The English revolution of the seventeenth century had abolished only the feudal ties of the great magnates, leaving those of the peasants intact. Copyhold was not recognised as the peasants' property and so the basis was laid for their later expropriation and 'landlordism'. The French Revolution of 1789, on the other hand, decisively destroyed the entire feudal structure and unleashed violence, not against the peasantry (as in England) but against the feudal – i.e. seigneurial – aristocrats. And not only did it liberate the peasants from all feudal ties, but it also expanded their total holdings by the division of commons and the sale of the *biens nationaux* [31].

This ingenious theoretical exercise, which had the outstanding merit of both confirming the French Revolution as a bourgeois revolution at the same time as it elevated the role of the masses at the expense of the bourgeoisie itself, was eagerly taken up by Albert Soboul and his pupils. Soboul's own methodological odyssey, at each stage along the way according more importance to the peasants, has been chronicled by Christof Dipper: in his general history of the Revolution, published in 1962, Soboul just remarked that within the general framework of the Revolution there developed a peasant current; in 1969 he was still writing only of a 'bourgeois revolution' in which 'the popular classes have been the motor'; but in 1971 he stated that 'the peasants and the popular revolution in fact stood at the centre of the bourgeois revolution and drove it forwards'; in his review of Ado's book he went so far as to abandon the phrase 'bourgeois revolution' in favour of 'peasant-bourgeois revolution'; finally, in 1978, he went the whole hog and called it a 'peasant revolution' which had forced a bourgeois revolution in the countryside and thus opened the way for capitalism [41].

No great acumen is required to spot that Ado and his

French supporters have 1917 just as much as 1789 in view. That is why Lenin rather than Marx has proved so much more helpful as a source of supportive theoretical quotations. Ado does his gallant best to enlist the support of the master and Soboul has exclaimed testily: 'For my part, I have never considered *Das Kapital* to be the Bible nor Marx to be a prophet. One will always find quotations of Marx, Engels, Lenin and – why not? – Stalin and Mao, to oppose to other quotations' [15; 30]. Significantly, Soboul made that observation in the course of berating Marxist heresy.

But no matter how much ingenuity is exercised in selecting what to quote and what to explain away, the obstinate fact remains that Marx had a very low opinion of peasants. In his view, the peasant was doomed just because he was a peasant, his imminent demise an inevitable consequence of progress and not to be regretted, for the peasant was engaged in 'the most primitive and irrational form of exploitation'. An economy based on peasants was bound to make the people chained to it 'a class of barbarians', 'uniting in itself all the crudeness of primitive social forms with all the tortures and all the misery of modern society'. No amount of planing and smoothing can make observations by Marx such as the following fit the Ado–Soboul version of the French Revolution: 'The evil to which the French peasant is succumbing is just his dwarf-holding, the partition of the soil, the form of tenure which Napoleon consolidated in France' [8].

As Soboul observed, Marxist scripture should not be treated as if it were Holy Writ, least of all by an agnostic. However, there are more substantive objections to be raised against the notion of a peasant revolution that was really bourgeois. So much of the peasant activity after 1789 was explicitly *counter*-revolutionary in character that the gap between subjective perceptions and objective roles is stretched much too far to be credible. Significantly, Soboul and his followers have paid virtually no attention to the counter-revolution, which has been placed by revisionists at the very centre of the stage, a mass movement comparable in scope to the Revolution itself [129].

The Marxists have a fair point when they stress that what really matters about late-eighteenth-century 'feudalism' is the meaning attached to it by contemporary peasants and not its actual (and minimal) relationship to its medieval ancestor [10]. But they then inflate its scope and meaning well beyond anything those peasants would have recognised. As one regional study after another has demonstrated, the insurgents were not just revolting against feudalism (or rather the seigneurial system) and even where they did so, it was not so much the seigneurial dues themselves to which they took exception as their commercial exploitation. They rose not against a reactionary feudal aristocracy but in defence of a pre-capitalist economic system based on small peasant holdings and against the tendency towards agrarian capitalism displayed by their seigneurs, an increasing number of whom were urban bourgeois [48; 53]. In short, the peasant revolution was not for capitalism but against it.

Against the seductive argument that this last conclusion is valid only on a subjective level and that 'objectively' – in spite of themselves – the peasants were on the side of progress, it is necessary only to consider the actual development of French agriculture in the following century. What Ado and his followers fail to take into account is the inescapable fact that the peasants freed from the fetters of feudalism wanted nothing more than self-subsistence and sought to avoid the risks involved in commercial farming. Moreover, and *objectively*, the opportunities for most of them were strictly limited by the old obstacle of poor communications. It was not until the transport revolution, which began in the middle of the nineteenth century with the construction of the railways, that the opportunity to specialise and the incentive to produce a marketable surplus were created. Agricultural production was probably lower in 1820 than it had been in the 1780s [131].

As Maurice Garden has observed, until the Second Empire the agrarian history of France in the nineteenth century was largely a repetition of the eighteenth century: only the railways and the concentration of population in towns brought change. They, not the Revolution of 1789, were the real destroyers of the old regime in the country [46]. The legislation of the Revolution had changed the legal status of the peasants – and may even have improved the material status of the minority lucky enough to own their own land – but on the way of life and way of thinking of the great mass of the rural population, it had had no effect.

If the Revolution neither established nor accelerated but probably delayed the development of capitalism in France [25], a closer look at the social dimension also raises doubts about its radicalism. On the face of it, the abolition of the nobility, the abolition of the seigneurial regime, the abolition of venality, the expropriation of the *émigrés*, the introduction of egalitarian legal codes and the establishment of a meritocracy should have led to a change of elites. In the event, once the turmoil of the mid-1790s had died down, it turned out that there had been little change. When, in 1802, Napoleon's prefects compiled the electoral lists which in effect were surveys of local notables, they established that most of the wealthiest landowners in France were still the nobles of the old regime [132]. Recanting an earlier view, Robert Forster has commented: 'large landlords of the Old Regime, noble or not, were not destroyed – nor even permanently hurt – by the Revolution' [137]. Napoleon may have talked about a field-marshal's baton in every private's knapsack, but in practice he preferred to rely on men of independent and well-established means. The only major change he made to the traditional structure was to increase the number and improve the status of civil servants. The result was that the mixed elite of nobles and commoners which had been in the process of formation during the eighteenth century was now firmly established. As Robert Forster has concluded:

The elite that governed France after the Revolution and owed so much to the conscious policies of Napoleon was essentially a notability of landlords and *hauts fonctionnaires*, with smaller contingents of lawyers, merchants, and manufacturers – smaller in both number and influence. This elite was drawn from the old noble families as well as from newcomers, a successful amalgam of wealth, education, family connections, local influence, and political power. Without legal privileges and placing less weight on birth, it saw itself as a service elite, the rule of the *capacités*. Drawn from many of the same families who had administered France in the Old Regime, the new notables evolved

55

a common set of social values and attitudes that were appropriate to their own time and place. They governed France, with a few brief interruptions, from 1800 to 1880 and even beyond. [137]

One is tempted to append the comment *Plus ça change, plus c'est la même chose* but this would be too immobile a note on which to end. The Revolution did have an enormous impact, although it was more a revolution in the mind than a revolution of reality. It remains topical right down to the present day, as an ideal of political liberty and social justice and as a model for overthrowing an established order. However imperfectly realised at the time, the revolutionary principles did revolutionise the way in which each succeeding generation viewed politics and society. With the possible exception of the Russian Revolution of 1917, no episode has had such a universal and enduring impact as the French Revolution. Yet when one cuts through the political rhetoric to reach the social and economic foundations of France, its actual impact turns out to have been relatively modest. As it was a political revolution with social consequences, rather than a social revolution with political consequences, it is hardly surprising that it modified rather than destroyed the old regime. As William Doyle has suggested, in his conclusion to his volume in this series, substantial elements of the old regime lingered on even into the twentieth century.

Select Bibliography

There is space to list only those works actually cited in the text, together with a handful of others found particularly useful. The next step for the student should be the bibliography in [129].

Historiography

[1] W. Doyle, *Origins of the French Revolution* (1980). This admirably concise and lucid study supersedes all previous historiographical surveys.
[2] R. Reichardt, 'Bevölkerung und Gesellschaft Frankreichs im 18. Jahrhundert: Neue Wege und Ergebnisse der sozialhistorischen Forschung 1950–1976', *Zeitschrift für historische Forschung*, IV (1977). A long, full and very valuable bibliographical survey.

Marxist and Marxist-Leninist interpretations

[3] F. Furet, *Marx et la Révolution française* (1986). A study of Marx's writings on the French Revolution, accompanied by appropriate texts by Marx.
[4] M. Grenon and R. Robin, 'A propos de la polémique sur l'ancien régime et la Révolution: pour une problématique de la transition', *La Pensée*, CLXXXVII (1976). Lively polemical attack on revisionists such as Chaussinand-Nogaret and Furet, but also critical of Soboul.
[5] G. Lefebvre, *The coming of the French Revolution* (1947). Still one of the best introductions to the subject.
[6] ——, *The French Revolution*, 2 vols (1962). First published fifty years ago, it remains stimulating and informative.
[7] ——, 'The place of the Revolution in the agrarian history of France' in R. Forster and O. Ranum (eds), *Rural society in France* (1977). Unlike Soboul, sees the peasants in 1789 as essentially conservative.
[8] D. Mitrany, *Marx against the peasant: a study in social dogmatism* (1951).
[9] E. Schmitt and M. Meyn, *Ursprung und Charakter der Französischen Revolution bei Marx und Engels* (1976). A very helpful account and

analysis of the views of Marx and Engels on the French Revolution.

[10]   A. Soboul, *La Civilisation et la Révolution française* (1970). The definitive statement of Soboul's views on the Enlightenment and the Revolution.

[11]   ——, 'Classes and class struggles during the French Revolution', *Science and Society*, XVII (1953). A convenient summary of Soboul's early views.

[12]   ——, *The French Revolution 1787–1799. From the Storming of the Bastille to Napoleon* (1974). The most accessible work by Soboul in English but superseded by his later work.

[13]   ——, 'L'historiographie classique de la Révolution française', *Historical Reflections – Réflexions historiques*, I (1974). Perhaps the most thoughtful of Soboul's replies to the revisionists.

[14]   ——, 'Problèmes théoriques de l'histoire de la Révolution française, *La Nouvelle Critique*, XLIII (1971).

[15]   ——, 'Sur l'article de Michel Grenon et Régine Robin', *La Pensée*, CLXXXVII (1976). Critical of a Marxist but 'gradualist' view of revolution.

[16]   ——, 'Sur le mouvement paysan dans la Révolution française', *La Pensée*, CLXVIII (1973). Summarises and commends the views of Anatoly Ado.

[17]   V. P. Volguine, 'L'idéologie révolutionnaire en France au XVIIIe siècle: ses contradictions et son évolution', *La Pensée*, LXXXVI (1959). Trenchantly expressed views of a Soviet historian.

Revisionist criticism

[18]   G. Chaussinand-Nogaret, 'Aux origines de la Révolution française: noblesse et bourgeoisie', *Annales ESC*, XXX (1975). One of the most trenchant attacks on Marxist orthodoxy.

[19]   A. Cobban, *The Social Interpretation of the French Revolution* (1964). The Wiles lectures of 1962, which became the most important single manifesto of the revisionists.

[20]   E. Eisenstein, 'Who intervened in 1788?', *American Historical Review*, LXXI (1965). Has one important point to make.

[21]   W. Doyle, 'Was there an aristocratic reaction in pre-revolutionary France?', *Past and Present*, LVII (1972). A very important piece; argues convincingly that there was none.

[22]   G. Ellis, 'The "Marxist interpretation" of the French Revolution', *English Historical Review*, XCIII (1978). A penetrating and effective critique.

[23]   F. Furet, *Interpreting the French Revolution* (1981). This collection of articles includes his celebrated attack on [10].

[24]   C. Lucas, 'Nobles, bourgeois and the origins of the French Revolution', *Past and Present*, LX (1973). This has proved to be one of the most influential of the revisionist attacks.

[25] E. Schmitt, introduction to his anthology *Die Französische Revolution* (1977).

[26] G. V. Taylor, 'The bourgeoisie at the beginning of and during the Revolution' in Eberhard Schmitt and Rolf Reichardt (eds), *Die Französische Revolution – zufälliges oder notwendiges Ereignis?* (1983). Argues that the Revolution was due to the coincidence of a political crisis with a socio-economic crisis.

[27] ——, 'Noncapitalist wealth and the origins of the French Revolution', *American Historical Review*, LXXII (1967). A very important article which argues that there was more in old regime France to unite the nobility and bourgeoisie than to divide them.

[28] ——, 'Types of capitalism in eighteenth century France', *English Historical Review*, LXXIX (1964).

[29] ——, 'Bourgeoisie' in Samuel F. Scott and Barry Rothaus (eds), *Historical dictionary of the French Revolution 1789–1799*, vol. I (Westport, C. T., 1984). Helpful discussion of possible definitions.

See also [115(b), (c) and (d)].

The Ancien Régime

[See also the bibliography in William Doyle's *The Ancien Régime* (1986) published in this series]

Economy and society

[30] A. Ado, *Krest'yanskoe dvizhenie vo Frantsii vo vremya velikoy burzhiaznoy revoliutsii kontsa XVIII veka* (1971). An imaginative Marxist-Leninist work on the peasant revolution which has exerted a strong influence on Albert Soboul and his pupils.

[31] ——, 'Krest'yanskie vosstaniya i likvidatsiya feodal'nykh povinnostey vo vremya frantsuzkoy burzhuaznoy revoliutsii kontsa XVIII v.' in M. Kossok (ed.), *Studien über die Revolution*, 2nd edn (1971). A short article, but easier to obtain than [30], which is something of a bibliographical rarity.

[32] ——, 'Le mouvement paysan et le problème de l'égalité (1789–1794)' in A. Soboul (ed.), *Contributions à l'histoire paysanne de la Révolution française* (1977). Unfortunately for those who do not read Russian, not a summary of [30].

[33] C. B. A. Behrens, 'Government and society' in E. Rich and C. Wilson (eds), *The Cambridge Economic History of Europe*, vol. V (1977). A penetrating and wide-ranging essay, which places France in its European context.

[34] ——, 'Nobles, privileges and taxes in France at the end of the Ancien Régime', *Economic History Review*, XV (1962–3). Argues that despite

formal exemptions, the French nobility *were* taxed.

[35]   L. Bergeron, 'L'économie française sous le feu de la Révolution
       politique et sociale', in P. Léon (ed.), *Histoire économique et sociale du
       monde*, vol. III: *Inerties et révolutions (1730–1840)* (1978).

[36]   D. Bien, 'La réaction aristocratique avant 1789: l'exemple de l'ar-
       mée', *Annales ESC*, xxix (1974). Much wider-ranging than the title
       suggests; shows how easy it was to become a noble in old-regime
       France.

[37]   M. Bloch, 'La lutte pour l'individualisme agraire dans la France du
       XVIIIe siècle', *Annales ESC*, ii (1930). Still very important for
       understanding why French agriculture changed so little during the
       eighteenth century.

[38]   F. Braudel and E. Labrousse (eds), *Histoire économique et sociale de la
       France*, vol. II: *1660 à 1789* (1970), vol. III: *L'avènement de l'ère
       industrielle (1789–années 1880)* (1976).

[39]   G. Chaussinand-Nogaret, *The French nobility in the eighteenth century:
       from feudalism to enlightenment* (1985). A brilliant blend of insights and
       polemics.

[40]   F. Crouzet, 'England and France in the eighteenth century: a com-
       parative analysis of two economic growths' in R. M. Hartwell (ed.),
       The causes of the industrial revolution in England (1967). Shows that
       France was not so far behind England in 1789 in terms of industrial-
       isation as has been often supposed.

[41]   C. Dipper, 'Die Bauern in der französischen Revolution', *Geschichte
       und Gesellschaft*, vii (1981). A very useful bibliographical review.

[42]   W. Doyle, *The Ancien Régime* (1986). Lucid and cogent essay, particu-
       larly strong on the historiography of the old regime.

[43]   ——, *The old European order 1660–1800* (1978). Excellent general study
       which puts France in a European perspective.

[44]   J. Dupâquier, *La population française aux XVII et XVIIIe siècles* (1979).
       The most authoritative review of the fragmentary evidence relating
       to French population in the period.

[45]   R. Forster, 'The middle classes in eighteenth century Western Euro-
       pe' in J. Schneider (ed.), *Wirtschaftskräfte und Wirtschaftswege: Festschrift
       für Hermann Kellenbenz*, vol. III (1978). A very helpful discussion of
       what 'bourgeois' meant to contemporaries.

[46]   M. Garden, 'Un procès: la "révolution agricole" en France', as in [35].
       Shows how limited was agricultural change in eighteenth-century
       France.

[47]   P. Goubert, *L'Ancien Régime*, 2 vols (1962, 1973). English translation
       of vol. I available. Particularly good on the social and economic
       aspects of the old regime.

[48]   G. van den Heuvel, *Grundprobleme der französischen Bauernschaft
       1730–1794* (1982). A short, but penetrating and very helpful survey.

[49]   E. Hinrichs, E. Schmitt and R. Vierhaus (eds), *Vom Ancien Régime
       zur Französischen Revolution. Forschungen und Perspektive* (1978). An
       exceptionally valuable collection of conference papers.

[50]   O. Hufton, *The poor of eighteenth century France* (1974). A masterpiece of social history.

[51]   ——, 'The seigneur and the rural community in eighteenth century France. The seigneurial reaction: a reappraisal', *Transactions of the Royal Historical Society*, 5th series, XXIX (1979). Demonstrates that the seigneurial system had its positive side.

[52]   V. Hunecke, 'Antikapitalistische Strömungen in der Französischen Revolution', *Geschichte und Gesellschaft*, IV (1978). Thoughtful, but not an easy read; particularly good on the peasants.

[53]   E. Le Roy Ladurie, 'Révoltes et contestations rurales en France de 1675 à 1788', *Annales ESC*, XXIX (1974). An exceedingly valuable review article which discusses monographs by Saint-Jacob, Poitrineau, Meyer and others.

[54]   P. Masson, *Histoire du commerce française dans le Levant au XVIIIe siècle* (1911).

[55]   J. Meyer, 'La noblesse au XVIIIe siècle: aperçu des problèmes', *Acta Poloniae Historica*, XXXVI (1977). Argues, among other things, that Chaussinand-Nogaret has underestimated the number of nobles in old regime France.

[56]   M. Morineau, 'Was there an agricultural revolution in eighteenth century France?' in R. Cameron (ed.), *Essays in French economic history* (1970). Answers: no, there was not.

[57]   W. M. Reddy, *The rise of market culture. The textile trade and French society, 1759–1900* (1984). A major study, much wider in range than the title suggests.

[58]   H. Sée, *La France économique et sociale au XVIIIe siècle*, 4th edn (1946). Still useful.

[59]   A. Soboul, 'La Révolution française' in [38] vol. III.

[60]   J. Tarrade, *Le commerce colonial de la France à la fin de l'ancien régime*, 2 vols (1972).

Government and politics

[61]   D. Richet, *La France moderne: l'esprit des institutions* (1973). A short work but contains all manner of arresting insights; particularly good on the political crisis of the late 1780s.

[62]   C. B. A. Behrens, *Society, government and the Enlightenment: the experiences of eighteenth century France and Prussia* (1985). A revealing comparison of two very different states.

[63]   J.-P. Bertaud, *La Révolution armée. Les soldats-citoyens et la Révolution française* (1979). Full of interesting and surprising information.

[64]   J. Bosher, *French finances 1770–1795: from business to bureaucracy* (1970). Overturned previous explanations of the financial problems of the monarchy.

[65]   J. Bromley, 'The decline of absolute monarchy' in J. Wallace-Hadrill and J. McManners (eds), *France: government and society*, 2nd edn (1970). A stimulating essay which stresses the destabilising role of the Parlements.

[66]   A. Cobban, *A History of Modern France*, vol. I (1961). Out of date in some respects but still valuable *faute de mieux*.

[67]   W. Doyle, 'The price of offices in pre-revolutionary France', *Historical Journal*, XXVII (1984). An original and very important article which shows, among other things, that the price of office was not declining in the eighteenth century.

[68]   ——, *The Parlement of Bordeaux and the end of the old regime 1771–1790* (1974).

[69]   ——, 'The Parlements of France and the breakdown of the old regime 1771–1788', *French Historical Studies*, XIII (1970). Argues persuasively that Maupeou's reforms were essentially a political manoeuvre to discredit Choiseul.

[70]   D. Echeverria, *The Maupeou Revolution: A study in the history of libertarianism, France, 1770–1774* (Baton Rouge, 1985). Argues cogently that the last four years of Louis XV's reign marked a turning-point for the old regime.

[71]   J. Egret, *Louis XV et l'opposition parlementaire* (1970). The standard account; indispensable to an understanding of the political history of France in the eighteenth century.

[72]   V. Gruder, *The Royal Provincial Intendants: a governing elite in eighteenth century France* (1968).

[73]   E. G. Léonard, *L'armée et ses problèmes au XVIIIe siècle* (1958). Sheds much light on a neglected but very important topic.

[74]   P. Mathias, 'Concepts of revolution in England and France in the eighteenth century', *Studies in Eighteenth Century Culture*, XIV (1985). A very illuminating comparison of the fiscal systems of the two countries.

[75]   J. Revol, *Histoire de l'armée française* (1929).

[76]   J. Shennan, *France before the Revolution* (1983). An excellent concise introduction to the period.

[77]   ——, *The Parlement of Paris* (1968). Lucid and authoritative account of the main centre of political opposition to the old regime monarchy.

[78]   Herman Weber, 'Das Sacre Ludwig XVI vom 11. Juni 1775 und die Krise des Ancien Régime' in [419]. An interesting and important article on the old-fashioned nature of Louis XVI's kingship.

[79]   S. Zweig, *Marie Antoinette* (1933). Despite its age, still essential for a proper understanding of an apparently frivolous but crucial aspect of the old regime's fate.

The Enlightenment

[80]   L. Althusser, *Montesquieu, Rousseau, Marx. Politics and History* (1982). Unorthodox and stimulating Marxist analysis.

[81]   K. M. Baker, 'French political thought at the accession of Louis XVI', *Journal of Modern History*, L, 2 (1978). Complements [78] in an enlightening way.

[82]   ——, 'On the problem of the ideological origins of the French

Revolution' in Dominick L. Capra and Steven L. Kaplan (eds), *Modern European intellectual history: reappraisals and new perspectives* (Ithaca, N.Y., 1982).

[83] R. Chartier, 'Culture, lumières, doléances: 'les cahiers de 1789', *Revue d'histoire moderne et contemporaine*, xxviii (1981). Judicious review of the evidence for and against a connection between the Enlightenment and the *cahiers de doléance* of 1789.

[84] H. Chisick, *The limits of reform in the Enlightenment. Attitudes towards the education of the lower classes in eighteenth century France* (1981). Shows, among other things, that most enlightened thinkers did not want to see the masses educated beyond their station.

[85] R. Darnton, *The business of enlightenment. A publishing history of the Encyclopédie 1775–1800* (1979). Much of this monumental study is rather technical but the last fifty pages or so are of more general interest.

[86] ——, 'The high enlightenment and the low-life of literature in pre-revolutionary France', *Past and Present*, li (1971). Influential and revealing examination of the radical gutter-press of pre-revolutionary France.

[87] ——, 'In search of Enlightenment: recent attempts to create a social history of ideas', *Journal of Modern History*, xliii (1971).

[88] ——, 'Reading, writing and publishing in eighteenth century France: a case-study in the sociology of literature', *Daedalus*, c (1971). Includes some spicy illustrations of the pornographic *libelles* in circulation before the Revolution.

[89] F. Furet and W. Sachs, 'La croissance de l'alphabétisation en France (XVIIIe–XIXe siècle)', *Annales ESC*, xxix (1974). Wide-ranging and informative review of the current state of knowledge.

[90] P. Gay, *The Enlightenment, an interpretation*, 2 vols (1967, 1969). Elegant, wordy, Whig account of the Enlightenment.

[91] ——, *Voltaire's Politics* (n.d.) The best of Gay's books, it relates the development of Voltaire's political thought to his response to specific incidents.

[92] ——, 'Why was the Enlightenment?' in P. Gay (ed.), *Eighteenth century studies* (1975). Sharply critical of Marxist interpretations of the Enlightenment.

[93] J. Godechot, 'Nation, patrie, nationalisme et patriotisme en France au XVIIIe siècle', *Annales historiques de la Révolution française*, xliii (1971). Important examination of the way in which the meaning attached to words such as 'nationalism' and 'patriotism' changed in the course of the eighteenth century.

[94] L. Goldmann, *The philosophy of the Enlightenment* (1973). Short, odd but stimulating advocacy of a dialectical approach to the Enlightenment.

[95] N. Hampson, 'The Enlightenment in France' in R. Porter (ed.), *The Enlightenment in national context* (1981). An essay full of sharp insights and telling comparisons between France and England.

[96] J. Lough, *The contributors to the Encyclopédie* (1973). Demonstrates that

a wide cross-section of both upper and lower classes were involved.

[97] ——, *The Encylopédie* (1971). Helpful guide to the most important single publication of the French Englightenment.

[98] ——, *The Philosophes and post-revolutionary France* (1982). Argues that most philosophes would have approved of most of the reforms achieved between 1789 and 1791.

[99] D. Mornet, *La pensée française au XVIIIe siècle* (1969). Contains a convenient summary of his much longer *magnum opus* on the intellectual origins of the Revolution.

[100] D. Richet, 'Autour des origines idéologiques lointaines de la Révolution française: élites et despotisme', *Annales ESC*, xxiv (1969). Stresses the importance of the role played by the nobility in the development of the Enlightenment and of liberalism.

[101] D. Roche, 'Milieux académiques provinciaux et société des lumières', *Livre et société dans la France du XVIIIe siècle*, vol. I (1965). Provides valuable statistical information on the social composition of three important provincial academies.

[102] D. Roche, 'Die "Sociétés de pensée" und die aufgeklärten Eliten des 18. Jahrhunderts in Frankreich' in H. Gumbrecht, R. Reichardt and T. Schleich (eds), *Sozialgeschichte der Aufklärung in Frankreich*, vol. I (1981).

[103] R. Shackleton, *Montesquieu, a critical biography* (1961). Particularly illuminating on the social context of the Enlightenment in France.

[104] C. G. Stricklen, 'The *Philosophe's* political mission: the creation of an idea, 1750–1789', *Studies on Voltaire and the Eighteenth Century* (1971). Complements [69] and [70] in arguing that the period around 1770 marked a turning-point in the fortunes of the old regime.

[105] M. Vovelle, 'La sensibilité pré-révolutionnaire' in [149]. Contains important observations on the growth of literacy and dechristianisation in pre-revolutionary France.
See also [115(a)].

The Final Crisis

[106] J. Egret, *The French Pre-Revolution* (1977). The essential starting-point for any investigation of the political crisis of the late 1780s.

[107] G. Lefebvre, 'The movement of prices and the origins of the Revolution' in J. Kaplow (ed.), *New Perspectives on the French Revolution* (1965). Essential for an understanding of the socio-economic crisis of the late 1780s.

[108] J. McManners, 'The Revolution and its antecedents' in [165]. Deals with the period after 1774.

[109] S. Scott, *The response of the royal army to the French Revolution. The role and development of the line army 1787–1793* (1978). Very important for understanding why the old regime collapsed when it did.

[110] L.–P. Comte de Ségur, *Mémoires*, 3 vols (1824–6). A good sample

of the huge memoir literature available.

[111] G. V. Taylor, 'Revolutionary and non-revolutionary content in the *cahiers* of 1789: an interim report', *French Historical Studies*, VII (1972). Argues persuasively that the Revolution produced the revolutionaries, not the other way round.

[112] M. Vovelle, *The fall of the French monarchy, 1787–1792* (1983). Intelligent but not consistently lucid defence of the Revolution as essentially bourgeois.

[113] D. Wick, 'The court nobility and the French Revolution: the example of the Society of Thirty', *Eighteenth Century Studies*, XIII (1980). Demonstrates the predominantly noble character of the revolutionary leadership in 1789.

The Revolution

[114] T. C. W. Blanning, *The origins of the French Revolutionary wars* (1986). Examines the origins of the revolutionary wars of the 1790s.

[115] A. Cobban, *Aspects of the French Revolution* (1968). Collected essays and articles; see especially (a) 'The Enlightenment and the French Revolution' (b) 'The myth of the French Revolution' (c) 'Political versus social interpretations of the French Revolution' and (d) 'The French Revolution: orthodox and unorthodox interpretations'.

[116] F. Crouzet, 'Wars, blockade and economic change in Europe 1792–1815, *Journal of Economic History*, XXIV (1964). Should be read in conjunction with [40].

[117] A. Forrest, *Society and politics in revolutionary Bordeaux* (1975). One of the best regional studies.

[118] F. Furet and D. Richet, *The French Revolution* (1970). Lively revisionist account; also very well-illustrated.

[119] N. Hampson, *The Terror in the French Revolution* (1981). Short but penetrating pamphlet.

[120] P. Higonnet, *Class, Ideology and the Rights of Nobles during the French Revolution* (1981). Odd but stimulating.

[121] L. Hunt, *Politics, culture and class in the French Revolution* (London, 1986). Not an easy read, but original and rewarding.

[122] M. Hutt, *Chouannerie and counter-revolution. Puisaye, the princes and the British government in the 1790s*, 2 vols (1983).

[123] G. Lefebvre, *The Thermidorians and the Directory* (1964). Still the best readily available political narrative.

[124] G. Lewis, *The second Vendée. The continuity of counter-revolution in the Department of the Gard, 1789–1815* (1978) Consistently fascinating account of counter-revolutionary agitation in the South-East.

[125] M. Lyons, *France under the Directory* (1975). Organised thematically, it sheds much light on many neglected aspects of a much-neglected period.

[126] J. McManners, *The French Revolution and the Church* (1969). Concise, penetrating study of a relationship of central importance.

[127] W. Scott, *Terror and repression in revolutionary Marseilles* (1973).

[128] A. Sorel, *Europe and the French Revolution*, vol. I (1969). A true classic, still well worth reading, especially for its emphasis on the primacy of foreign policy.

[129[D. M. G. Sutherland, *France 1789–1815. Revolution and counter-revolution* (1985). Particularly good on the counter-revolution, which is placed on an equal footing with the Revolution itself.

[130] D. Woronoff, *The Thermidorean regime and the Directory 1794–1799* (1984). More chronological in organisation, it admirably complements [125].

The aftermath

[131] J.–C. Asselain, *Histoire économique de la France du XVIIIe siècle à nos jours*, vol I: *De l'Ancien Régime à la Premiére Guerre Mondiale* (1984). The best up-to-date French survey.

[132] L. Bergeron, *France under Napoleon* (1981). Excellent modern account of the domestic side of Napoleon's empire.

[133] R. E. Cameron, 'Economic growth and stagnation in France 1815–1914' in B. Supple (ed.), *The experience of economic growth* (1963). Examination of the problems besetting French industrialisation in the nineteenth century.

[134] R. E. Cameron, 'A new view of European industrialisation', *Economic History Review*, 2nd series, xxxviii (1985). Argues that the French road to industrialisation – a long slow process – was normal for Europe.

[136] F. Crouzet, 'Les conséquences économiques de la Révolution', *Annales historiques de la Révolution française*, xxxiv (1962). Illustrates the detrimental consequences of the Revolution for the French economy.

[137] R. Forster, 'The French Revolution and the "new" elite' in J. Pelenski (ed.), *The American and French Revolutions* (1980). Stresses the continuity of the traditional French elites.

[138] D. R. Leet and J. A. Shaw, 'French economic stagnation 1700–1960', *Journal of Interdisciplinary History*, viii (1977/8). Argues that the reputation of the French economy for backwardness is undeserved.

[139] R. Magraw, *France 1815–1914: The bourgeois century* (1983).

[140] P. O'Brien and C. Keyder, *Economic growth in Britain and France 1780–1914* (1978). Demonstrates, among other things, the retardative effects of the Revolution on the agrarian structure of France.

[141] R. Price, *The Economic Modernisation of France* (1975). The importance of communications is the *leitmotiv* of this consistently informative and stimulating study.

[142] C. Trebilcock, *The Industrialisation of the Continental Powers 1780–1914* (1981). Excellent modern survey, particularly good in explaining and applying models of industrialisation.

[143] J. Tulard, *Napoleon. The myth of the saviour* (1984). The best modern

study; each section concludes with a very helpful review of the literature and current controversies.

[144] E. Weber, *Peasants into Frenchmen. The modernisation of rural France 1870–1914* (1977). A brilliant book, which shows – among other things – how much of the old regime had survived into the late nineteenth century.

Index